C000214693

FASTING

Dag Tessore

FASTING

New City
London

First published as *Il Digiuno*
© 2006 by Città Nuova, Rome

First published in Great Britain 2007 by
New City
Unit 17, Sovereign Park
Coronation Road
London NW10 7QP

© 2007 English Translation New City London

Translated by Frank Johnson

Cover design Tomeu Mayans
Picture © Barry Redmond

British Cataloguing in Publication Data:
A catalogue reference for this book is available from the British Library

ISBN 978 1 905039 02 09

Typeset by New City London
Printed and bound in Great Britain by Cromwell Press, Trowbridge, Wiltshire

Contents

A Note from the Editor

The practice of fasting has been present in the earliest religious traditions and in the Christian Church from its beginning, from the time of Jesus himself, in fact. Fasting, however, has also evolved and changed over the centuries, affected as it was by local custom and culture and by different interpretations in various Christian traditions. The vast majority of the content of this book is based on Scriptural and Patristic material, with some references to Roman Catholic and Orthodox teaching and practice. To offer a more complete view of the subject, the author was happy for there to be an Anglican perspective.

Thus we start with the following foreword by the distinguished Anglican theologian and member of the Anglican-Roman Catholic International Commission (ARCIC II), Nicholas Sagovsky.

Foreword

In the Summer of 2006, the Archbishop of York, John Sentamu, pitched his tent in a side-chapel at York Minster and spent a week fasting and praying for peace in the Middle East. He was doing exactly what this little book commends. As an Anglican, brought up in Uganda, he was reminding his fellow-Anglicans of a practice we have largely forgotten but which is integral to the discipleship of many Christians in the developing world, where they know so much more about what it is to be hungry.

Dag Tessore has written an ecumenical text. He draws on ancient Christian sources which are important for Christians of East and West. As a lifelong Anglican, I recognise much of what he says because it is reflected so strongly in my own tradition. The key Anglican sources all commend the practice of fasting, both individual and corporate. The *Book of Common Prayer* (1662) lists as 'Vigils, Fasts, and Days of Abstinence' the eve of sixteen major feasts, and as 'Days of Fasting or Abstinence' the forty days of Lent; the Ember

Days (three days of prayer in each season, when we pray for those to be ordained); the three Rogation Days (days of prayer for a fruitful harvest); and all the Fridays of the year, except Christmas Day. In the proposed Book of Common Prayer (1928) a new rubric was inserted before the Order of the Holy Communion: 'It is an ancient and laudable custom of the Church to receive this Holy Sacrament fasting. Yet for the avoidance of all scruple, it is hereby declared that such preparation may be used or not used, according to every man's conscience in the sight of God.' Anglicans have always been reluctant to lay down the law about how we should fast.

Guidance about fasting was given to Christians in the Church of England by the two-part homily 'Of Good Works; and First of Fasting' in the second *Book of Homilies* (1571) of which John Jewel (1522-71) was the author.[1] Fasting is commended as a 'good work' but in no way one that merits salvation. Study of Scriptural examples, of which there are many, shows that fasting is 'of two sorts; the one outward,

1. *Certain Sermons or Homilies Appointed to be Read in Churches in the time of Queen Elizabeth of Famous Memory* (London: SPCK, 1938), pp. 291-310.

pertaining to the body; the other inward, in the heart and mind'. So, 'that we ought to fast is a truth more manifest than that it should have need to be proved; the Scriptures which teach the same are evident'. Three aims are given for fasting: 'to chastise the flesh, that it may not be too wanton, but tamed and brought in subjection to the spirit'; 'that the spirit may be more fervent and earnest in prayer'; 'that our fast may be a testimony and witness with us before God of our humble submission to his high Majesty, when we confess and acknowledge our sins unto him'.

Amongst classic Anglican writers, Richard Hooker (?1554-1600) defends the Church's observance of set fasts by reference to Scripture and the Church Fathers, showing both how there can be too much insistence on fasting (Tertullian) and too little (Arius).[2] This is not, he insists, a matter on which churches should be divided. After listing a string of good reasons for fasting, his final one is, 'that every man may be every man's daily guide and example as well by fasting to declare humility as by praise to express joy in the sight of God'.

2. Ecclesiastical Polity V.lxxii (*The Works of Mr Richard Hooker*, Oxford: Clarendon, 1865, vol. II, pp. 128-45).

Hooker's concern that rules and regulations about fasting should not become a source of division is echoed in the poem *Lent* by George Herbert (1593-1633):

> Neither ought other men's abuse of Lent
> Spoil the good use; lest by that argument
> We forfeit all our Creed.[3]

In the same poem Herbert is, however, clear about the Lenten obligation to fast: 'The Scriptures bid us fast; the Church says *Now*.' In *A Priest to the Temple* he gives a picture of the fasting observed by his idealised seventeenth century country parson:

> The Parson in his house observes fasting days: and particularly, as Sunday is his day of joy, so Friday his day of Humiliation, which he celebrates not only with abstinence of diet, but also of company, recreation, and all outward contentments ... . *Now fasting Days contain a triple obligation; First,* of eating less that day, than on other days; *Secondly,* of eating no pleasing, or over-nourishing things, as the

3. *The Works of George Herbert in Prose and Verse (London: Bell and Daldy, 1859), vol. II, p. 91.*

> Israelites did eat sour herbs; *Thirdly,* of eating no flesh.[4]

As far as the last is concerned, however: 'Meat was made for man, not man for meat': there may well be situations where it would be right to eat meat whilst observing the fast.

With so many set days of fasting in the Anglican year, this was a popular theme amongst preachers. At the end of the seventeenth century, William Beveridge (1637-1708) recommended 'keeping the body under by fasting, and so bringing it into subjection to the soul'.[5] 'Fasting', he said, 'doth conduce much to our being holy but it cannot make us so.' He chose examples from Scripture, like those of Moses, Elijah and Jesus, to show that 'the greatest discoveries that God hath made of Himself to man, and the most powerful effects of the Spirit upon them, have usually been when they were fasting, and so in a right disposition for them.'

In many parts of the Anglican Communion similar – or even more emphatic – sermons can be heard today, but rarely, I guess, in England. The new Church of

4. *Ibid.*, vol. I, p. 185.
5. 'The Usefulness of Fasting', quoted in P.E. More and F.L. Cross, *Anglicanism* (London: SPCK, 1962), pp. 583-98.

England Prayer Book, *Common Worship*, no longer speaks of Days of Fasting but 'Days of Discipline and Self Denial'.[6] Fasting has largely become a matter of personal choice. Sermons about fasting, or locally observed fasts, often make the connection between the largely token fasting of Christians in the developed world and the shocking reality of world hunger. In England, Christians will sometimes accept the challenge of living at the income levels of the poorest in society. The focus of fasting is often (and rightly) on solidarity with the poor.

The Archbishop of York's fast reminded us of truths deep within the traditions of the Church: fasting as a means of repentance; fasting as a means of deepening prayer; fasting because we 'hunger and thirst' to see right prevail. This little book provides a timely reminder of these truths. Some of what it claims about the benefits of fasting is open to question (and, with the prevalence in Western cultures of eating disorders, it is especially important to fast wisely), but who can doubt the wisdom of committed, regular fasting in a consumerist society obsessed with food and self-gratification?

6. *Common Worship* (London: Church House Publishing, 2000), p. 531.

This book presents that challenge to each one of us. A Lenten prayer, written by Eric Milner-White (1884-1963), Dean of York, has helped me to respond:

> Lord let me fast most truly and profitably, by feeding in prayer on thy Spirit; reveal to me myself in the light of thy holiness.[7]

May this book be a timely challenge to all its readers, 'revealing to us ourselves', and drawing us closer to one another as, through times of fasting, we draw closer to Christ.

Nicholas Sagovsky
Canon Theologian, Westminster Abbey

7. E. Milner-White, *My God My Glory* (London: SPCK, 1959), p. 21.

Introduction

All the world's religions are familiar with the concept of fasting. The ancient Greeks fasted in the period of the Eleusinian Mysteries and the Thesmophoria, as well as on the occasion of liturgical ceremonies in the temple. The Egyptians practised abstinence from meat and wine for the Cult of Isis. The Romans too observed public fasts for religious reasons. Even the Zoroastrians, who explicitly declared themselves to be against fasting and abstinence, in fact had some fast days in their calendar. In Confucianism and the Aztec religion the practice of fasting and abstinence from certain foods was commonplace. The practice of fasting is also to be found among the African peoples, the South American Indians and the Australian aboriginals. In fact, it is often in those places where there is extreme poverty and a shortage of food where fasting is practised most rigorously.

In Buddhism and Hinduism fasting is one of the most important aspects of their ascetical way. Still today Buddhist monks must not eat anything between midday and dawn of the following day. Muslims fast between sunrise and sunset for the whole of the month of Ramadan, and on the many other fast days during the year. The Qur'an and the whole religion of Islam give such weight to the practice of fasting as an aspect of physical and spiritual asceticism, penance and love for God, that it is one of the Five Pillars of the Islamic faith. In Judaism, public and private fasting have remained essentially the same as in Biblical times.

And what of Christianity? What did Jesus have to say on the subject? Did the Apostles and the early Christians fast? When, from the second to the fifth centuries, the Fathers of the Church, through their writings and the various councils, were defining the doctrine of Christian faith, what did they have to say about fasting? What meaning did fasting have in Christian spirituality down the centuries? And, more generally, what was the role of food and drink in the Christian view of life? We will try to answer these and many other questions in this little book. We will also try to rediscover the genuine Christian meaning of fasting in order to offer the contemporary Christian the chance to re-acquire this great spiritual and ascetical treasure offered to us in the Biblical and Patristic tradition. We will do all of this while respecting the teaching and the spirit of the Second Vatican Council.

Whilst wanting to present something simple and informative, nevertheless it seems important also to enrich the text with many Biblical and Patristic quotations. In fact, when tackling this subject, as St John Cassian said, "We will not be speaking about it ourselves, but we will say what has been passed down to us by the Holy Fathers".[1]

The reader will see that we refer very frequently to the Fathers of the Church, much more than to modern texts. This is a deliberate choice. St Augustine, St Basil, and the other great Fathers, are in fact those who laid the foundations of Christian doctrine and practice. On the subject of fasting, what they have written remains the basis for the continuing spirituality and life of the Church. So, if medieval and modern writers are quoted only rarely it is because we prefer to draw directly on the original sources.

1. John Cassian, *Ad Castorem pontificem de octo principalibus vitiis*, I (Greek version).

Chapter 1

Fasting as a Way of Returning to God

The practice of fasting, that is, abstaining from all food, or from certain foods, for a given period of time, is universal. There are very few religions or cultures, either ancient or modern, in which fasting does not exist. The religion of the Bible is no exception. In the Old Testament there are many references to fasting (*som*, in Hebrew). Let us have a look at some of these references and what the context is.

Not eating, even for just one day, is painful and exhausting, and in fact, fasting is always associated with suffering. It comes as no surprise therefore, that in the Old Testament, fasting is an expression of pain, of suffering. For example, when Elijah prophesied to the evil King Ahab about all the disasters that were to fall upon his perverse tribe, the king "tore his clothes, put on sackcloth and fasted" (1 Kings 21: 27; cf also Nehemiah 1: 4).

In the Bible, and in almost all religions, fasting is also a sign of mourning. On the death of Saul, David and his men "mourned and wept, and they fasted till evening because Saul and Jonathan his son and the army of the Lord and the house of Israel had fallen in battle" (2 Samuel 1: 12; cf 2 Samuel 3: 35; Judges 20: 26). On the occasion of Saul's funeral they fasted for seven days (cf 1 Samuel 31: 13; 1 Chronicles 10: 12).

In fact it is quite natural that on the death of a loved one, those left behind feel that to start immediately feasting and gorging on food is not appropriate. The death of a loved one causes us to suspend our normal daily routine for a while, and leads us to reflect on another, more serious, dimension. The sorrow and the emotions that accompany the death of a loved one often help us forget, at least for a moment, our own needs and pleasures.

If we spontaneously mourn and fast when someone dear to us has died or is suffering, it is easy to understand why Israel felt she had to weep and to fast when her most dearly beloved, God, was suffering. This is why, for example, when Moses sees the sins of the people and the love of God injured and offended, he says: "Then I lay prostrate before the Lord as before, for forty days and forty nights; I neither ate bread nor drank water, because of all the sin you had committed, provoking the Lord by doing what was evil in his sight" (Deuteronomy 9: 18). Here fasting means: while the others are eating and drinking and offending God with their various sins, I love you, I want to be near you and share in your bitterness and your sorrow. Thus, in the Old Testament, fasting on the Day of Expiation, once a year, was instituted; a day when the whole people was obliged to fast in remembrance of the many offences committed against God during the year (Leviticus 23: 27-32). On that day, the Bible says, "you will mortify yourselves".

Other similar concepts can be found throughout the Bible. Warned by the prophet Jonah, "the people of Nineveh," repentant and sorrowful for having sinned against God, "believed in God; they proclaimed a fast... No human being or animal, no herd or flock, shall taste anything. They shall not feed, nor shall they drink water" (Jonah 3: 5-7). In fact, the fast of the Ninevites is still practised today, once a year, in the Coptic Church, as a sign of repentance and conversion to God. The prophet Daniel also says, "Do penance," and then goes on to explain what this means: "I had eaten no rich food, no meat or wine had entered my mouth" (Daniel 10: 2-3).

To abstain from food for three days, like the Ninevites, or from rich foods for three weeks, like Daniel, or to practise any other form of mortification through fasting, expresses the disposition of the soul which repents of its errors and sins and wants to be reconciled with God. As God himself says, through the mouth of Joel: "Yet even now, says the Lord, return to me with all your heart, with fasting, with weeping, and with mourning" (Joel 2: 12).

There are many cases quoted in the Bible of very pious people who, feeling inadequate before the immense love of God, fasted "every day" (in other words, they only had one meal a day, and ate only frugally: one such example would be Judith (Judith 8: 6), and another the prophetess Anna (Luke 2: 37). Fasting, says St Ambrose, is *"humilitas mentis"*[1]: [lowliness of mind] physical abstinence from food, with the resultant feeling of hunger, suffering and tiredness, and is translated automatically, on the psychological level, into an attitude of humility and sincere repentance. An authentic prayer to God, a sincere pleading to the Almighty, presupposes "a humble spirit and a contrite heart; but whoever eats rich foods cannot have a humble spirit and a contrite heart. Thus it is obvious that prayer without fasting is weak and shallow. Whoever wants to pray for

1. Ambrose, *De Elia et ieiunio*, VIII (22).

anything, will have fasting as a support in his prayer"[2]. "Repentance without fasting is useless," says St Basil.[3]

Also in this perspective, the Church views fasting as a "punishment", as a penance imposed by the confessor on the believer who has sinned: "impose healthy fasts, as long as they are not fatal"[4] is an effective way of helping the penitent to feel sorrow for his sins and urge him towards a more sincere repentance.

Ambrose also says that fasting is *"sacrificium reconciliationis"*[5] [a sacrifice of reconciliation]. In what sense? What is a sacrifice? In the Old Testament, sacrifice means renouncing voluntarily something we like, value or find useful, and offering it to God. For example they sacrificed animals, choosing the healthiest and best: man owned them; they were his by right. He could get a good price for them; he could use them to work on the land; he could get milk or wool from them; he could slaughter them and he and his family could eat them;

2. John Chrysostom (attributed to), *Opus imperfectum in Matthaeum, XV.*
3. Basil, *De ieiunio sermo 1,* III.
4. The Council of Toledo (397-400), can. VII; cfr. Council of Tours (567), can. XIX.
5. Ambrose, *De Elia et ieiunio,* IX (31).

but instead he took them to God's Temple and gave them away, for nothing. And what was more, often, when a holocaust was being offered, not only the person offering the animal was deprived of it, but no one got any benefit from it, not even the priest of the Temple. In fact the beast was completely burnt on the altar and nothing remained. In this way no human use or advantage could be gained from the sacrifice. So, why was it done? To give witness, through this act, which humanly speaking was absurd, that a God exists. According to biblical faith, God commanded these sacrifices to see if man believed in him, or if he was capable of doing something that makes sense only if God really exists.

Giving up something voluntarily therefore, especially food, applies to both sacrifice and to fasting: in both cases a person deprives themselves of something essential for their life to "understand that one does not live by bread alone" (Deuteronomy 8: 3). Also, with regard both to sacrifice and fasting, man, in his attempt to return to God repentant and converted, renounces those material goods and those pleasures which, often, were the cause of his going away from God in the first place. By renouncing them, he recognises that such things did not satisfy him and admits that God is worth much more.

So, fasting expresses repentance and conversion: but not just fasting. Fasting is often combined with other forms of mortification: weeping, wearing sackcloth and ashes, lying prostrate on the ground can all be found in the Bible, and not just in the Old Testament. When Israel wishes to avert God's anger and avoid his punishment, she turns to similar forms of repentance. There are many examples of this: Psalm 35: 13; Jeremiah 14: 12; Esther 4: 3; 2 Maccabees 13: 12; etc. Here we quote from Judith 4: 9-13: "And every man of Israel cried out to God with great fervour, and they humbled themselves with much fasting. They and their wives and their children and their cattle and every resident alien and hired labourer and purchased slave – they all put sackcloth around their waists. And all the Israelite men, women, and children living at Jerusalem prostrated themselves before the temple and put ashes on their heads and spread out their sackcloth before the Lord. They even draped the altar with sackcloth and cried out in unison, praying fervently to the God of Israel not to allow their infants to be carried off and their wives to be taken as booty, and the towns they had inherited to be destroyed, and the sanctuary to be profaned and desecrated to the malicious joy of the Gentiles. The Lord heard their prayers and had regard for their distress; for the people fasted for many days throughout Judea and in Jerusalem before the sanctuary of the Lord Almighty." This passage is a very good illustration of the biblical concept and practice of fasting.

Here we note another important aspect of fasting, according to the Bible, an aspect which, like others, is passed on quite naturally, to Christianity: the public and communitarian nature of fasting. "Blow the trumpet in Zion; sanctify a fast; call a solemn assembly!" (Joel 2: 15). In fact, the community of believers is not just a collection of individuals; it is a "mystical body". This is why both Jewish and Christian feasts are by their very nature communitarian. It is the whole people that celebrates the feasts of the Lord, and the whole people that mortifies itself and fasts together. As a matter of fact, the Bible often makes the point that on days of penance all "people and animals" must fast (cf Joel 3: 7).

The union and interconnection between the different members of the mystical body that is Israel, and then later, the Church, also explains the practice of "fasting for others". Esther asks the Jews in exile to "hold a fast on my behalf" (Esther 4: 16). And vice-versa, Moses fasts for his sinful people, who in the meantime were eating and enjoying themselves, in order to avert God's anger. Similarly, to Christians it is said: "Bless those who curse you, pray for your enemies, fast for those who persecute you."[6]

We have said that fasting, as repentance and conversion to God, also helps ward off divine punishment and the calamity that that brings with it. So, we are talking about a way of gaining God's favour. In some cases this brings about a sincere proposal of conversion and renunciation of sin. Samuel, for example, to avoid defeat in the imminent battle against the Philistines, ordered the whole people to fast and "They fasted that day, and said, 'We have sinned against the Lord'" (1 Samuel 7: 2-6; cf 2 Chronicles 20: 3). Also Judas Maccabaeus and his men fasted to obtain victory in battle (2 Maccabees 13: 12), but their fast was undoubtedly a sincere expression of repentance and love for God. Esther fasted in order to obtain God's protection in her hazardous task of presenting herself to King Ahasuerus (Esther 4: 16). Samuel too, in order to procure victory in battle, forbade anyone to eat: "He had laid an oath on the troops, saying, 'Cursed be anyone who eats food before it is evening and I have been avenged on my

6. *Didache*, I, 3; cf Mt 5: 44.

enemies.' So none of the troops tasted food" (1 Samuel 14: 24).

In other cases one can say that fasting was used as a simple instrument for obtaining divine protection, without it necessarily being accompanied by adequate humiliation of the heart: when his son became gravely ill, David "pleaded with God for the child; David fasted, and went in and lay all night on the ground", to obtain a cure for him. But when the child died, David stopped fasting: "While the child was still alive," he said, "I fasted and wept; for I said, 'Who knows? The Lord may be gracious to me, and the child may live.' But now he is dead; why should I fast?" (2 Samuel 12: 6-23).

Although Jesus was strongly opposed to the idea of fasting in order to obtain favours from God, or as a religious practice divorced from sincere conversion of heart, he was in fact a great master of fasting. As we know, he fasted for forty days in the desert (which we will come back to later on), and he spoke about this important subject on various occasions. The first Gospel passage we want to consider in this regard is Mark 2: 18-20 (cf Matthew 9: 14-15 and Luke 5: 33-35): "Now John's disciples and the Pharisees were fasting; and people came and said to him, 'Why do John's disciples and the disciples of the Pharisees fast, but your disciples do not fast?' Jesus said to them: 'The wedding-guests cannot fast while the bridegroom is with them, can they? As long as they have the bridegroom with them, they cannot fast. The day will come when the bridegroom is taken away from them, and then they will fast on that day." The bridegroom is, of course, Christ himself. What he meant was that his disciples couldn't fast right then during the happiest and most joyful moment in the history of humanity, when God incarnate had come down into their midst to bring them the Good News of their redemption. In fact, the incarnation of Jesus meant that God, despite all the sins and betrayals of his people, still had mercy on them: he decided to forgive them all and to break the bonds of damnation. This is why the disciples could not fast in his presence. It was the moment of reconciliation between God and man: it was the time "to eat and celebrate" (cf Luke 15: 23).

From all this we can understand why, in the Christian tradition, fasting is prohibited on feast days. Already in the Old Testament, there was no fasting on the Sabbath and on "the festival days of the house of Israel" (Judith 8: 6). In the same way, right from the early times, the Church decreed that no Christian should fast on Sunday[7]:

7. Cf Council of Gangra (345), can. XVIII; Augustine, *Epistolae*, XXXVI, 12 (29); Council of Braga (563), can. IV.

it was to be a day of joy, in the knowledge that "the bridegroom is with us". Also, from the early centuries of the Church right up to the present time, there was, in principle, no fasting for the fifty days between Easter and Pentecost:[8] on those days we celebrate the victory of Christ over death and sin. It would be incorrect, or more accurately, offensive, to mourn on feast days.

However, Jesus added: "The day will come when the bridegroom is taken away from them, and then they will fast on that day". And when was the bridegroom taken away? – Principally on the day of his passion and death, Good Friday. This is why, right from the earliest times, the Church has celebrated this day with a particularly austere fast[9]. But obviously, the whole of Holy Week, and especially the Triduum (Maundy Thursday, Good Friday and Holy Saturday) is part of this deep mourning for Christ. How can we not mourn and fast when the Bridegroom, the Beloved, the Lord and Saviour is taken from our midst, betrayed, arrested, insulted, vilified, beaten and finally, crucified?

8. Cf Augustine, *Sermones,* CCX, 1 (2); Jerome, *Epistolae,* XLI, 3; John Cassian, *Collationes,* XXI, 19-20; Egeria, *Iterarium,* XLI; Council of Tours (567), can. XVIII.
9. Cf Tertullian, *De oratione,* XVIII.

Many give witness to the fact that in the early centuries of Christianity rigorous fasting was observed for the whole of Holy Week.[10] The *Constitutiones apostolorum*, written around the fourth century, clearly affirm: "He himself [Jesus] commanded us to fast for these six days".[11] The same text continues telling us how to carry out this solemn and sacred fast, although we know from other sources that, as we shall see, fasting was practised in all sorts of different ways in the Church, with no uniformity whatsoever: "During the days of the Easter [=Holy Week] fast, from the Monday to the Friday, and Saturday as well – six days – eating only bread, salt, and vegetables, drinking water; abstain from wine and from meat. These are in fact, days of mourning, not feast days. On the Friday and the Saturday, however, a total fast – for those who are strong enough – not eating anything until midnight [of Easter Sunday]."[12]

We have already mentioned that there were no binding, universal rules governing the times and ways of fasting. What counted

10. Cf Irenaeus, Letter to Pope Victor, quoted in Eusebius of Cesarea, *Historia ecclesiastica*, V, 24,12; Dionysius of Alexandria. *Epistola ad Basilidem*, can. I.
11. *Constitutiones apostolorum*, V, 15.
12. *Ibid.* V, 18.

was the sincere spirit of mourning for the dd recognition of the fact that his bitter Passion was caused by our sins, and a real yearning for conversion. If this spirit exists, there is no need for rules to establish for how long we should fast and which foods we should not eat: each person does what they can, according to their physical limitations and their love for Christ. "Rejoice in so far as you are sharing Christ's sufferings" (1 Peter 4: 13). The Fathers of the Church frequently emphasise that fasting is not an end in itself, nor is it a formal duty which has to be fulfilled. In the Old Testament there is only one "official" fast, which is binding: the Day of Expiation, to which we have already referred; only after the exile in Babylon were other public fasts added: cf Zechariah 7: 5; 8: 19; Esther 9: 31.

Also, the actual practical methods of fasting in the Bible differed from one time to another: on some occasions fasting meant not eating anything at all for three consecutive days (cf Esther 4: 16; Tobit 3: 10-11 (Vulgate); 2 Maccabees 13: 12). On other occasions they abstained from eating "rich foods" and from meat and wine, for three weeks (Daniel 10: 2-3). The same thing applied to Christianity: sometimes there were three days of uninterrupted, total fasting (the so-called *triìmero,* still today practised in the Orthodox Churches, especially by priests and monks, for the first three days of Lent). Other times it was just one day, when one ate nothing until evening time, and again on other occasions fasting consisted in not eating before three in the afternoon, the Ninth Hour, the time Christ died on the cross.[13] Then there were fasts which consisted of eating just one meal a day and abstaining from meat, wine and other foods. Erma, writing around 140 A.D. says: "On fast days I will eat nothing but bread and water."[14] And of St Anthony, Athanasius says that his fasting consisted of eating only in the evening and only bread, salt, and water.[15]

It is clear, therefore, that the rules and practices varied tremendously, as Cassian and the historian Socrates inform us in the fifth century[16]; but it is equally clear that when they spoke of fasting, they were speaking about something very serious, austere and demanding. Not only were the fasts of the early Church many, taking up many days in the year, as we shall see, but also the ways in which they were practised went beyond the simple "going without lunch or

13. Cf Tertullian, *De ieuinio*, II and X; Benedict of Nursia, *Regula*, XLI.
14. *Erma, Pastor*, III, 5, 3.; cf *Canones Hippolyti*, XX-XXI.
15. Athanasius, *Vita Antonii*, VII.
16. Cf John Cassian, *Collationes*, XXI, 24-30; Socrates, *Historia ecclesiastica*, V, 22.

supper", or "abstaining from meat". In the early Latin Church, just as today in the Eastern Orthodox Church, all the faithful, clergy and lay people, fasted. For example, during Lent, for approximately forty days, they ate one meal a day, and that after Vespers. And for the whole of Lent they abstained, not only from eating meat, but also from milk and dairy products and eggs, as well as often from fish, wine and oil. Some communities and individual Christians held even stricter fasts, but all had the same basic aims, those of purifying the body and of being detached from material things, as well as expressing an authentic love for Christ and a genuine desire to share in his Passion.

We have mentioned Lent, the period of penance and fasting *par excellence*. Right from the earliest times, the Church saw in the forty days preceding Easter, or in the forty days preceding Holy Week, (according to the different traditions of East and West) as a time particularly suited to conversion of the heart, prayer, penance and, of course, fasting, in preparation for Easter. Lent was also linked[17] with the three celebrated forty-day fasts reported in the Bible: that of Moses before receiving the tablets of the Law on Mount Sinai (cf Exodus 34, 28);

17. Cf Maximus of Turin, *Sermones*, XVIII.

that of Elijah, before going to Mount Horeb, where he had a vision of God (cf 1 Kings: 19: 8); and finally, that of Jesus himself, when the Gospel tells us he "was led by the Spirit in the wilderness, where for forty days he was tempted by the devil. He ate nothing at all during those days" (Luke 4: 1-2).

The pilgrim Egeria, in the fourth century, confirms the practice of fasting during Lent, although different methods were used[18] (many in Palestine, she says, took "only water and a little gruel"[19] during the whole of Lent). The Council of Laodicea, also in the fourth century, states: "Fasting must be done for the whole of Lent, eating frugally [i.e. no meat, eggs, milk, etc.]"[20] "In this most sacred time of Lent, no one should eat lunch, except on Sundays", writes St Augustine.[21] He added that not to observe the Lenten fast "is a sacrilege".[22]

St Maximus of Turin writes: "Violating Lent and ignoring the sacred fast, proclaimed by the Lord, is no light matter. In fact it is written: 'Whoever wishes to remain in Christ

18. Egeria, *Itinerarium,* XXVII, I and XXVIII, 1-3.
19. Ibid. XXVIII, 4. This is also laid down in *Canones Hippolyti, can. – XX-XXI.*
20. Council of Laodicea, can. L.
21. Augustine, *Sermones suppositi,* CXLII, I.
22. Augustine, *Sermones suppositi,* CXLVII, I.

has to walk the path he has commanded' (1 John 2: 6). So, if you want to be a Christian, you must do what Christ did. He, who was without sin, fasted for forty days, and you who are a sinner, don't want to do the Lenten fast?"[23]

It is clear, therefore that the Lenten fast centred on the person of Christ and his redeeming death. But it is equally clear that Lent is a time of conversion, of turning to God, of rethinking, of repentance; it is a time to reflect on the direction of one's own life, on the meaning of one's existence; it is a chance to stop and to ask – Where I am I going? What is the point of the things I am doing, my work, my pastimes, my commitments? What is the point of it all? What place does God have in my life?

I can also think about whether my going to church and my praying are sincere, or if they have become just an empty routine. Thus fasting can help not only purify the body, but also make the soul more clear, more placid, and, as a result, more able to concentrate on and think about God. Fasting and prayer have always gone together in the Church (cf Acts 14: 23): fast days are days of prayer, says St Ambrose.[24]

23. Maximus of Turin, *Homiliae*, XL, 3-4.

Although Lent is the time of penance par excellence, in that it is linked to mourning the passion and death of Christ, other periods or days in the year have also assumed, in the Christian tradition, a penitential character. We will take a brief look at them now.

Three days of the week are specially linked to the Passion: Wednesday, Friday and Saturday. The Wednesday and Friday tradition probably goes back to the apostles themselves. The religious Jews at the time of Jesus normally fasted on Mondays and Thursdays (cf Luke 18: 12). The apostles, on the other hand, chose Wednesdays and Fridays in memory of Jesus' betrayal by Judas and the death of Christ. As it says in an ancient text: "The canonical fasts, that is Wednesdays and Fridays, must not be ignored, except for a serious reason: it was in fact Wednesday when Judas decided to betray the Lord; on Friday the Saviour was crucified. It is obvious, therefore, that not to fast on Wednesday or Friday, except for grave reasons, is as if we have betrayed the Lord together with the traitor and as if we have crucified him with those who crucified him".[25]

24. Ambrose, *De Elia et ieiunio,* X (34).

Already in the I century A.D. the Didache prescribes: "Fast on the Fourth Day [Wednesday] and the Preparation [Friday]".[26] Numerous ancient Greek and Latin sources confirm that both in the Eastern and Western Church on these two days a rigorous fast was observed, throughout the year, apart from joyful and festive occasions such as Pentecost, by both lay people and clergy.[27] Although the form and manner of the fast differed from place to place, all Christians considered the Wednesday and Friday fasts as sacred and inviolable, on the same level as that of the Lenten fast. This is still the case in the Orthodox Church, although not all lay people observe the fast: they eat just one meal on the fast day, after 15.00 hrs, and they abstain from

25. Apollonius Monachos, quoted in Rufinus of Aquileia, *Historia monachorum*, VII. Cf Corpus iuris canonici, *Decretum Gratiani*, III, 4, 16.

26. *Didache* , VIII, 1.

27. Cf Tertullian, *De oratione*, IX; *De ieuinio*, II and X; Egeria, *Itinerarium*, XXVII, 5; Augustine, *Epistolae*, XXXVI, 13 (30); Benedict of Nursia, *Regula*, XLI; Hyppolitus, *Traditio apostolica*, XXVIII; *Canones apostolorum*, LXIX; *Constitutiones apostolorum*, LXIX; *Constitutiones apostolorum*, V, 15 and 20; VII, 23; Peter of Alexandria, *Epistola canonica*, can. XV, 6; *Exposito fidei*, XXII; Origen, *In Leviticum homiliae*, X, 2 (according to Rufinus's translation), Epiphanius, *Adversus Haereses*, LXV, 6; Council of Tours (567), can. XVIII; etc.

eating meat, fish, dairy products, eggs, wine and olive oil. This mourning for Christ is regarded as so serious and such a duty, that even important and joyful solemnities such as the Assumption of the Blessed Virgin Mary, if they fall on a Wednesday or a Friday, have an element of mourning: they eat fish, but not meat, milk or eggs.

In the Latin Church on the other hand, observance of the fast on these two days (Wednesday and Friday) became more and more lax (see chapter 5) and round about the eleventh century all that remained as an obligation was the Friday fast, which was nothing like as austere as in the early centuries.

In recompense, however, the Latin Church, right from the earliest times (first or second centuries) established the Saturday fast, "as a sign of reverence for the burial of the Lord,"[28] Tertullian testifies to the fact that many Catholics in the Western Church observed the Saturday fast.[29] However, as the Eastern Church had established Saturday (the Sabbath) as a semi-feast day (because God stopped creating the world that day and sanctified the Sabbath)

28. Corpus iuris canonici, *Decretum Gratiani,* III, 4, 13.
29. Tertullian, *De ieiunio,* XIV.

and had categorically forbidden fasting on that day,[30] many of the Latin Fathers also maintained that Saturday should not be a fast day. St Augustine for example was strongly opposed to the Saturday fast, in conformity, he says, with "all the Eastern Christians and most of those in the West",[31] even though, he admits, "the Roman Church and several Western Churches" have done so, "through ignorance" as St John Cassian says in the fifth century.[32] Anyway, Rome preferred to keep to its tradition, even though it was in sharp contrast with the East: in 416 A.D. Pope Innocent I reaffirmed the obligation of the Saturday fast, and many other papal and conciliar decrees since then, right up to modern times, have followed suit.[33] In the eleventh century Peter Damian dedicated a booklet to the subject in which he criticises those who stick to the ancient tradition: "Should we be feasting when He is lying in the tomb?".[34]

However, above and beyond the disagreements between the Churches regarding the

30. Cf *Canones apostolorum,* LXIV; Egeria, *Itinerarium,* XXVII, 1.
31. Augustine, *Epistolae,* XXXVI.
32. John Cassian, *De coenobiorum institutes,* III, 10.
33. Innocent I, in *Decretum Gratiani,* III, 4, 13; Council of Agde (506), XII; IV Council of Orleans (541), can, II.
34. Peter Damian, *De ieiunio sabbati,* V.

Saturday fast, it is clear that all three fast days, (Wednesday, Friday and Saturday) are associated with mourning for the passion and death of Christ. In fact, all the sufferings and difficulties of the Christian life are a "sharing in the sufferings of Christ", as St Paul says, and in which our being disciples of the Crucified One is expressed "in toil and hardship, through many a sleepless night, hungry and thirsty, often without food" (2 Corinthians 6: 5; cf 2 Corinthians 11: 27).

Other days and during other periods of the year, however, were deemed fast days for other reasons. As fasting was an act of conversion to God, of purification of the body and the mind, and being in every sense a "good work", it soon became the norm to observe fasts of short or long duration, in preparation for the great Christian feasts. In particular there were:

The Advent Fast. Various Latin authors of the first millennium write about a fast lasting around forty days before Christmas. [35] The Byzantine Church still maintains this tradition (the Orthodox do not eat meat, eggs or

35. Cf. The Venerable Bede, *Historia ecclesiastica,* III, 27 and IV, 30; Isidore of Seville, *Regula monachorum,* XII; Rabanus Maurus, *De clericorum institutione,* II, 22.

dairy products between 15 November and 24 December); in the Latin Church the Council of Mâcon in 581 prescribed fasting every Monday, Wednesday and Friday from 11 November to Christmas Eve.[36] The latter practice was only partially observed and fell progressively into disuse.

Fast of the Assumption and other Vigils. An anonymous author of the fifth or sixth century writes that "a fast should be observed on the vigil of the great solemnities" and recalls the "canonical fasts", including "the Assumption of Holy Mary" and that of "the Holy Apostles Peter and Paul": "on these vigils," he writes, "we must always fast".[37] In the East they still observe a rigorous fifteen-day fast before important feasts.

Fast after Pentecost before the feast of the Holy Apostles [Ss Peter and Paul, 29 June]. This too is still observed in the Eastern Church, whereas it has disappeared in the West. Both Latin and Greek sources in the fifth century testify to this:[38] after the fifty

36. Council of Mâcon (581), can. IX; see also Council of Tours (567), can, XVIII.
37. Attributed to Augustine, *Sermones ad fratres in eremo commorantes*, XXV.

days following Easter during which, as already mentioned, there was never any fasting, a fast was established (for a few days, or a week or more, according to the different traditions) to continue the ascetical routine which had been interrupted, and to make a worthy preparation for the feast of Ss Peter and Paul at the end of June.

Fasts of the Ember Days at the Four Seasons. This was a specifically Western tradition which was still in force until the last century. It was a fast introduced by the Fathers, and one that went back to the Old Testament.[39] It consisted of fasting for three days (Wednesday, Friday and Saturday)[40] at the beginning of every season [weeks following 13 December, first Sunday in Lent, Pentecost, 14 September] in order to "consecrate" the whole year to God.[41] It was in use, especially in Rome, already in the fifth century.

Fast of Rogation-tide. This too is an exclusively Western fast which was observed

38. Cf *Constitutiones apostolorum*, V, 20; Leo I, *Sermones*, LXXXVIII (LXXVI); Council of Tours (567), can. XVIII.
39. Cf Leo I, *Sermones*, XV (XIV), 2; cf Zech 8: 19.
40.Cf Leo I, *Sermones*, LXXXVIII (LXXXVI), 5.
41. *Cf Ibid. XIX (XVIII), 5.*

until very recently. It was a three-day fast in preparation for the feast of the Ascension and consisted not only in abstaining from food, but also in penitential processions and litanies (call "rogations"). This fast was prescribed in 511 at the Council of Orleans.[42]

Finally we should mention another important form of fasting: the Eucharistic fast. "When, for the first time the Apostles received the Eucharist, they did not fast beforehand. Nevertheless, one cannot, for this reason, criticise the Church, which has always insisted on a Eucharistic fast. It was pleasing to the Holy Spirit that, out of reverence for this great Sacrament, the Body of the Lord should enter the mouth of the Christian before any other food. Thus this norm is observed everywhere".[43] St Augustine's testimony clearly shows us how well established the Eucharistic fast was. In fact it was in force before Augustine. Various texts of the third and fourth centuries attest to the existence of the "obligatory" fast before Holy Communion.[44] Successive Councils also reinforced this rule.[45]

42. I Council of Orléans (511), can. XXVII; 174.62cf Council of Tours (567), can. XVIII.
43. Augustine, *Epistolae*, LIV, 6 (7-8).

The mystery of the Eucharist has always been surrounded, in the Church, by great reverence and a great sense of the sacred. As it is the presence of God himself in our midst, it has always been thought inadmissible to receive the Eucharist without an adequate "purification" and only with great reverence: "You who wish to approach this tremendous and divine altar," writes St John Chrysostom, "and this sacred mystery, should do so in fear and trembling, with a pure conscience, with fasting and with prayer".[46] Such was the sacred respect for this Sacrament, that the Eucharistic fast was considered broken by even a tiny drop of water.[47] Some Fathers of the Church and some medieval ecclesiastical laws advise, or even prescribe, that the fast should be maintained for several hours after receiving the Body of the Lord.[48]

Abstention from all food and drink, including water, was the rule for the

44. Cf Hippolytus, *Traditio apostolica*, XXXVI; *Testamentum Domini Nostri*, II, 20 and 25; *Canones Hippolyti*, XIX and XXVIII; John Chrysostom, *In Epistolam I ad Corinthios*, XXVII (in I Cor 11: 17-28).

45. Cf II Council of Braga (572), can. X; Council of Auxerre (578), can. XIX; II Council of Mâcan (585),can. VI; VII Council of Toledo (646), can. II.

46. John Chrysostom, *In diem natalem Domini nostri Iesu Christi.*

47. Cf Timothy of Alexandria, *Responsio*, XVI.

48. Cf John Chrisostom, *In Epistolam I ad Corinthios*, XXVII, (in I Cor 11: 17-28).

Eucharistic fast in the Catholic Church until 1953, when Pope Pius XII allowed for the first time, beside medicine, water to be taken.[49] The length of the Eucharistic fast, in the Catholic Church, was gradually reduced: at the time of Thomas Aquinas a fast from midnight was established, in order to receive Holy Communion the next morning.[50] This rule remained in force,[51] apart from a few exceptions and dispensations especially in periods of disasters or war, until 1957, when Pius XII limited it to three hours before receiving Communion,[52] and finally, in 1964, Paul VI reduced it to one hour, which it remains today.

In the Orthodox Churches, on the other hand, things developed in the opposite direction, so to speak. Their extreme reverence for the Sacrament led them to extend the fast to three days before receiving Communion, and this is still observed in Russia, Serbia and Bulgaria. This custom however, albeit inspired by a great sense of devotion, has almost always led to a drastic reduction in the frequency of

49. *Pius XII, Motu proprio Sacram Communionem.*
50. *Thomas Aquinas, Summa theologica, III, 80, 8.*
51. *Cf Catechesimus Romanus, n. 230; Pius X, Catechismo Maggiore, n. 628.*
52. *Pius XII, Motu proprio Sacram Communionem.*

Communion. Many members of the Orthodox Church receive Holy Communion just three or four times a year, on solemn feast days.

The Eucharistic fast expresses people's respect for the Mass and for the extraordinary gift of the sacraments. Thus fasting accompanies other sacraments and not only the greatest of them, the Eucharist. The *Didache* in the first century tells us that before being baptised one had to fast,[53] and the Council in Trullo in the seventh century stipulates that priests, before conferring any sacrament, must fast.[54] In the Acts of the Apostles we read that St Paul, St Barnabas and others when "worshipping the Lord" and ordaining new ministers, fasted (Acts 13: 2-3).

So, we have seen how fasting, on the one hand expresses the sense of mourning for Christ, and of penance for sins, on the other hand it is a sign of fear, gratitude and reverence by human beings before God.

53. *Didache*, VII, 4.
54.Council in Trullo, can. XXIX; cf Basil, *De ieiunio sermo* I, VI.

Chapter 2

Separation from the Pagans or Fraternal Meal?

As we have seen, the Old Testament sanctions a series of dietary laws forbidding the Jews from eating certain meats (pork, hare etc.) that are deemed "impure" (cf Leviticus 11), and from certain combinations of foods, such as meat and milk together. These laws, which are still scrupulously observed by Orthodox Jews today, are extremely complex (the permitted food combinations can be calculated very precisely). The end result is that it is virtually impossible for a Jew to eat anything unless other devout, observant Jews have prepared it. Then, if we take into account the fact that a pious Jew will also observe fasts throughout the year, it is clear that these laws make it impossible for Jews to eat together with non-Jews. In fact, that was, and is, the aim of these laws which originate from the Bible. God did not want his chosen people to mix, to be "contaminated" by the "nations", or, in other words, with pagans. They were not to eat food prepared by pagans (cf Daniel 1: 8) or coming from pagan countries (cf Amos 7: 17; Hosea 9: 3), because, almost certainly, they do not respect the Mosaic dietary laws. But the basic reason for these dietary laws is to "distinguish" themselves from other peoples, to give witness to their radical difference, which is Abraham's faith in God. However, distinguishing oneself (by way of life, eating and dressing, etc.) from the pagans does not just have this symbolic connotation of the witness of faith, it is also to prevent the Chosen People from adopting those immoral habits that generally characterise atheist and pagan societies.

From this point of view, the early Christians and the Fathers of the Church were no less strict. St Paul warned Christians not to eat meat from pagan sacrifices (*eidolothyta*), not because it might contaminate them, but because to eat it would be a symbol of communion with the pagan world (cf 1 Corinthians 8 and 10: 19-33). "Do not even eat with such a one" (1 Corinthians 5: 11).[1] The risk was that one, especially one who was not very secure in their faith and on their spiritual pathway, might get

1. Clement of Alexandria, *Paedagogus,* II, 10, 6.

sucked into the (pagan) immoral lifestyle. In this sense, the advice of the Fathers not to expose oneself too much to the ways of a secularised society is still valid today, a society whose values are profoundly anti-Christian and contrary to the evangelical spirit of poverty, simplicity, modesty and meekness.

However, it is also clear that Christians cannot regard "pagan" society as an enemy, as a diabolical reality, because it is composed of human beings, created by God and redeemed by Christ, who are seeking, perhaps in the wrong way, happiness and truth, and therefore in the last analysis, God. So, if it is right to detest sin and sinful ways of life, we must never hate or despise those who are caught up in them; we must show them understanding, love and forgiveness. And our forgiveness cannot be based on a feeling of superiority on our part; the Old Testament, the Gospel and the Fathers make very clear on many occasions the moral superiority of certain pagans, publicans, prostitutes and sinners over the official members of the people of God! "If you fast for two days," says St Jerome, "don't think yourself better than those who have not fasted. You fast, but perhaps you lose your temper; another person eats, but is perhaps kind and gentle. With your anger you release the tension of the spirit and the hunger of your stomach, while the other eats in moderation and gives thanks to God".[2]

Also, the Christian is called to witness to faith in Christ, and therefore to evangelise. But this is impossible without respect for, acceptance of, and openness to, the other. Jesus said to the apostles: "Whenever you enter a town and its people welcome you, eat what is set before you" (Luke 10: 8), and the Patristic tradition is unanimous in encouraging Christians to "eat whatever is offered to you".[3] The example of numerous saints, who most certainly were not unused to austere fasts and mortification, show us that charity and hospitality should, almost always, take precedence over dietary laws, as long as it is really charity which motivates us, and not just a conscious or unconscious desire to ignore the fast. Anyway, St Basil says, we can be hospitable while offering the simplest of meals.[4] A story is told about the holy monk Moses who broke the fast and prepared some broth for some brothers who had come to visit him. When the other monks saw the spirit of charity that had moved the

2. Jerome, *Epistolae,* XXII, 37.
3. Clement of Alexandria, *Paedagogus,* II, 10, I.
4. John Cassian, *Collationes,* XXI, 14; *De coenoborium institutes,* V, 24.

Saint, they said to him: "Father Moses, you have broken man's law, but you have kept God's". Another anecdote of the Desert Fathers tells of a person who went to visit an anchorite, offering him something to eat in order that he would break his fast. "As he was leaving, the visitor said: 'Forgive me Father for having made you break your fast' but the monk replied: 'My rule is to make you welcome and send you on your way in peace'".[5] "In fact," says St Paul, "the kingdom of God is not food and drink, but righteousness and peace and joy in the Holy Spirit: If your brother or sister is being injured by what you eat, you are no longer walking in love. Do not let what you eat cause the ruin of one for whom Christ died!" (Romans 14: 17 and 15).

This subject becomes even more understandable when we consider that, for Christianity, unlike for Judaism, "there is nothing outside a person that by going in can defile" (Mark 7: 15). In other words there are no impure or prohibited foods. St Paul says that it is a heresy to "demand abstinence from foods which God created... What God has made

5. *Apophthegmata patrum,* (alphabetical series), Moses, V; *Apophthegmata patrum,* (thematic series), IX, 7.

clean, you must not call profane" (1 Timothy 4:3-5; cf Acts 10: 9-16). In contrast with the Jewish prohibition of certain types of meat and the Manicheans' despising of all things material and earthly, especially the flesh, for Christians, not only are all foods allowed, but they are sacred. This is why in the early Church they held a special ceremony where the bishop blessed fruits and vegetables,[6] and before every meal God's blessing is called down before starting to eat and God is thanked after having eaten (cf Acts 27: 35; Deuteronomy 8: 10).

If, during a meal, one abstained from certain foods (particularly meat, wine, etc), this is, the Fathers say, not because these things are impure or forbidden, but simply as an ascetical exercise to purify the body and the mind.[7]

Here we need to make a little clarification. The early Church, in fact, in line with the Old Testament, was of the idea that "meat with blood" and that from "animals killed by beasts or that have died naturally"[8] should be

6. Cf Hippolytus, *Traditio apostolica,* XXXI-XXXII.
7. Cf *Canones apostolorum,* LIII; Augustine, *Sermones,* CCVIII, I; Council of Braga (563), can. XIV.
8. *Canones apostolorum,* LXIII; reiterated by the Council of Gangra, can. II, and by the Council in Trullo, can. LXVII; cf John 9: 4; Lev 19: 26; 17: 15; Acts 15: 28-29.

"forbidden in themselves and always", as well as meat from sacrifices offered by pagans in their temples.[9] These laws, reaffirmed by various important Councils of the Church, remained in force in the Orthodox Churches. The Coptic Church of Ethiopia still observes all the dietary laws of the Old Testament. The Catholic Church, on the other hand, in the wake of St Paul's teaching, has always proclaimed that there are no forbidden foods and that even these meats are permitted.[10]

There is a danger in all of this, both in Judaism and in Christianity, namely that observance of the law can degenerate into Pharisaic formalism, and the true purpose of fasting is lost. In the Old Testament, God, speaking through the prophet Isaiah, says: "Look, you serve your own interest on your fast-day, and oppress all your workers. Look, you fast only to quarrel and to fight and to strike with a wicked fist... Is such the fast that I choose, a day to humble oneself? Is it to bow down the head like a bulrush, and to lie in sackcloth and ashes? Will you call this a fast, a

9. Cf *Constitutiones apostolorum*, VII, 21.
10. Cf Council of Florence, *Sessione* XI (1442); cf Francis of Assisi, *I Regula*, IX, 16.

day acceptable to the Lord? Is not this the fast that I choose: to loose the bonds of injustice, to undo the thongs of the yoke, to let the oppressed go free, and to break every yoke? Is it not to share your bread with the hungry, and bring the homeless poor into your house; when you see the naked, to cover them, and not to hide yourself from your own kin?" (Isaiah 58:3 7).

"What is the point," says St Maximus of Turin, "to be pale-faced through fasting if then you become livid with bitterness and envy? What is the point of not drinking wine, if then you become drunk with the poison of anger? What is the point of abstaining from meat, which was created to be eaten, whilst tearing your brothers limb from limb with malice and calumny?"[11] "As we fast with the stomach, so should we fast with the tongue, stopping ourselves from speaking malice, lies, nonsense, calumny and angry words".[12] "We should also make our hands fast, keeping them from hoarding and from greed. We should make our feet fast, so that we do not wander through the streets that lead us to see

11. Maximus of Turin, *Sermones*, XVIII; cf *Erma*, Pastor, III, 5, 1.
12. Dorotheus of Gaza, *Doctrinae*, XV, 4 (164).

indecent things. We should make our eyes fast, training ourselves not to gaze at beautiful faces and not to search for other hidden attractions...".[13] "You should know this my brothers, that if you do not forgive your enemies from your heart, everything, whether fasting or almsgiving or any other good deed, is useless".[14] "Exertions and fasts, without uprightness of heart, are useless and are more for outward appearance than for living a better life".[15]

Fasting has meaning if it is the sign of a true and sincere conversion of the heart to God (cf Jeremiah 14: 12; Joel 2: 12-13). It does not have any meaning if it is done merely out of habit or "tradition"; of such a fast God asks us: "Was it for me that you fasted?" (Zech 7: 5). Some people fast in order to diet or for medical reasons, others because they have overeaten and are nauseated by food, others to save money and others to show how pious and religious they are.[16]

Now we come to Jesus' teaching about fasting, reported in the Gospel: "And whenever

13. John Chrysostom, *De statuis,* III.
14. Attributed to Augustine, *Sermones ad fratres in eremo commorantes,* XLI.
15. Augustine, *De sancta virginitate,* XXXIV.
16. Attributed to Augustine, *Sermones ad fratres in eremo commorantes,* XLI.

you fast, do not look dismal, like the hypocrites, for they disfigure their faces so as to show others that they are fasting. Truly I tell you, they have received their reward. But when you fast, put oil on your head and wash your face, so that your fasting may be seen not by others but by your Father who is in secret; and your Father who sees in secret will reward you" (Mt 6: 16-18).

Jesus talks about hypocrites, and the subject of hypocrisy is very important with regard to fasting. We are talking here about fasting and its relationship with charity and almsgiving. How can we pretend, says St Augustine, to raise our prayers to God and beg his mercy and forgiveness, also through fasting, if we do not act mercifully to those in need of our mercy?[17] "How many poor people," he continues, "we could feed with the lunch we have not eaten today!"[18] Thus fasting can become a form of almsgiving, either as mercy for the poor to give them hope in the mercy of God, or as "social justice": giving back to the poor what we have taken away from them through our greed, our consumerism and our hedonism.

17. Augustine, *Sermones*, CCVII, 3.
18. Idem *Enarrationes in Psalmos*, XLII, 8.

"The abstinence of the person who fasts becomes the food of the poor person," says Pope Leo the Great.[19] Erma tells us what we should do in practice: "Work out how much you would have spent on the food you would have eaten that day and put it aside to give to the widow, the orphan, the needy person".[20] Eusebius of Alexandria, in line with all the other Fathers of the Church, goes so far as to say: "Whoever, having fasted, does not give his bread to the hungry, fasts in vain; fasting without sharing is useless".[21]

Today, at a time when there is perhaps a greater sensitivity to social justice and solidarity than there is to mortification and ascetical practices, it could be helpful to rediscover this value of fasting: to make a sacrifice for the poor and the hungry. In the early Church there was the custom of fasting precisely in order to put aside food and money for the needy.[22] In fact, it is quite different to give money or food to the poor, having experienced through fasting their feelings of

19. Leo I, *Sermones*, XIII, I.
20. Erma, *Pastor,* III, 5. 3; cf *Constitutiones apostolorum,* V, 20.
21. Eusebius of Alexandria, *Sermones,* I.
22. Cf Aristides, *Apologia,* XV, 9.

hunger and suffering, than to give them money or food while enjoying tasty food in abundance. Mother Teresa, speaking at a conference on world hunger, said that the public would have understood her talk better if they had not eaten for the whole day. "It is too easy for a master to teach about fasting with a full stomach!" said St Jerome.[23]

Fasting, in fact, should not just be a means of sharing hunger and bread with the hungry, but it should also be a way for us to learn how to live in a "poorer" way and to eat more simply. The Fathers of the Church have written thousands of pages describing and deploring the banquets of their times, almost always characterised by uncontrolled greed, waste, vulgarity and indecency. For Jesus too, banquets were the typical occasions in which the arrogance and the moral decadence of the rich was manifested (cf Luke 16: 19). But Christians are called to a healthy simplicity: their tables (not only on fast days) should be characterised by an authentic Christian "poverty". To rediscover the virtue of poverty is certainly one of the great challenges facing the Church in every

23. Jerome, *Epistolae*, LII, 7.

age. In current times, there is a great temptation to believe we are Christians and to pass as such, while at the same time our wardrobes and our bank accounts are overflowing, and we consider "normal" or "necessary" that which the Fathers would have called simply luxuries and fads.

This does not mean we should eat badly or sadly: "Is there not a healthy variety of foods even when eating simply?" writes Clement of Alexandria, "For example, we have onions, olives, vegetables, milk, cheese, fruit and all sorts of foods without adding sauces", nor are "sweets and honey" forbidden.[24] Even the simplest of foods can be good and tasty, in fact, it is they that are especially good because they are natural.

Even the most frugal of meals can be enjoyable when the whole family comes together to eat. Some of the practices St John Chrysostom suggests to the faithful, such as being silent while eating, or listening to a Bible reading,[25] can make a meal very beautiful and special. I myself recall, if the reader will forgive

24. Clement of Alexandria, *Paedagogus,* II, 15, 1-3.
25. John Chysostom, *In epistolam ad Ephesios,* XXI, I. Cf Hipploytus, *Traditio apostolica,* XXVIII.

me this personal digression, an occasion a few years ago, when I was staying with a close friend. He, his wife, their five children and two grandparents all lived in the same house in the country. It was a nice house, but quite small and poor. At lunchtime we all gathered around the large wooden dining table. My friend read a Psalm and, after having recalled the words of Jesus, "One does not live by bread alone, but by every word that comes from the mouth of God" (Matthew 4: 4), he read a passage from the Gospel and gave a blessing. It was a fast day and on the table, which was lit by a single oil lamp, there was water, barley bread, lentils, olives and quince purée, all exquisite products of the surrounding countryside. During the meal we alternated between calm and pleasant conversation, and silence. The silence was not embarrassing, but filled with peace and serenity. The grandmother added a drop of vinegar to her water "to remind us of the vinegar that was given to Christ on the cross," while the youngest child played with sticks of firewood, because he had no other toys. I don't recall ever having felt as happy as this in rich people's houses eating meat and watching television.

St Basil remarks how "fasting makes one enjoy and appreciate food more... slave to pleasure, don't you realise that you are cancelling out pleasure: the greed of the gullet in fact stops you from tasting the goodness of food. Nothing is as desirable as that which has not been made contemptible and boring by uninterrupted indulgence. Those things that one can only have rarely are much more enjoyable".[26]

What St Augustine said to his followers regarding fast days still has a certain relevance today: "Those who abstain from meat, but replace it with more sophisticated and more expensive dishes, are sadly mistaken. This is not 'abstinence', but 'exchanging sensual pleasures'". "On fast days," he continues, "we should spend less and give more to the poor".[27] Fasting has to be a genuine exercise in renunciation and poverty and consists in eating "just once a day and without reaching satisfaction"[28] those foods which we happen to have in or which we can buy cheaply, excluding meat, and also possibly, eggs and dairy products: the best thing is bread and water.[29] St Basil advises us to "choose whatever is easiest to find in a particular region and which costs little".[30]

26. Basil, *De ieiunio sermo* I, VIII.
27. Augustine, *Sermones*, CCIX, 3.
28. Peter Damascene, *Argumentum libri, De septem corporis actibus (in Philocalia).*
29. Jerome, *Epistolae*, LII, 12.
30. Basil, *Regulae fusius tractatae*, XIX, 2.

Chapter 3

Fasting as Mental Training

Let us now take a look at one of the most important aspects of fasting: its value as a mental discipline. To begin with it will be useful to look at the basic principles of "Christian psychology". According to Biblical and Patristic teaching, the human being is an indivisible unity of soul and body. And these two elements, soul and body, are not only united, but also strictly interdependent. The moods, the feelings, the sufferings of the human person are almost always psychophysical – in other words they involve both soul and body. For example, anger, desire, depression, boredom, as science shows us, are diseases of the soul, but at the same time of the body. In fact, they can be caused by imbalances in the nervous system, in the hormones, by taking certain drinks or drugs, by a lack of mineral salts or other substances, and so on. Our bodily organism has, therefore, a much more important role than we generally think, in relation to our mental peace and our "interior" life.

Those aspects which we normally regard as being purely mental, such as anger, sadness, happiness, etc., are actually "mechanisms" of our psychophysical organism. The mistake we often make is that of identifying ourselves with these impulses. If a chemical substance with a narcotic effect present in a certain food induces my stomach to long for that food and my nervous system transmits these stimuli to my brain, I am made to think: "I want this food; it is I who wants it." If an intensive advertising campaign perhaps using subliminal methods tells my mind that a certain product is desirable and necessary, I think: "I like that product; I think I need it; I want it." But what we don't realise is that this "I" and this "I want" are not our real "I", but merely psychophysical constructions conditioned by thousands of ephemeral external factors. In fact, what we presume is our "free will" is none other than a mechanical action based on various impulses and stimuli. So, where is the true "I" of the human person? It does exist, but to find it, we must stop identifying ourselves with these psychophysical processes, which the Fathers called "passions". When we start to recognise that "I am not my anger", "I am not my desire", "I am not these thoughts which pass through my mind", then and only then can we discover our authentic self, our true identity (heart, spirit, mind). Only then can we turn to God in prayer with a clear mind, which is not agitated or clouded by continual thoughts, distractions and images.

Thus, to free ourselves of these "passions", and above all, from identifying ourselves with them, is an important task for everyone, but especially for the believer who wants to have a mind capable of "thinking God". This "interior work", this "practice" this "training", as the Fathers call it, is often ignored and overlooked by Christians today. We often think that this is the stuff of "psychotherapy" or "Buddhist meditation". But, at the end of our discussion on fasting, we could not fail to remind ourselves of the importance of this aspect of the interior life of the Christian. In fact, fasting has always been understood by the tradition of the Church as an instrument of this "work".

The first step is recognising our dependence on impulses and passions and on how we are literally slaves of desires, pleasures, tastes, emotions etc. Often, for example, we want to give some time to some worthwhile activity (e.g. reading a book, praying, helping someone in need) but we don't manage to do it because our eating habit continually keeps us on a tight rein, telling us: "You must eat something," even if we have eaten just two hours before, and if we are about to eat a slice of bread, our gluttony tells us: "Only a slice of bread? Make yourself a nice dessert," and if you don't have all the ingredients, it says: "Go to the shop and buy them." And if when we get to the local shop, they don't have what we want, the voice says to us: "Get in the car and go to the supermarket", and so on. We want to read, we want to pray, but the "passions" have prevented us; it is they that govern us. We are not free persons.

We begin, therefore, to understand just how ridiculous it is to spend all that time and all that money to "service the stomach as if it were an implacable sovereign".[1]

We open our eyes, as St Clement of Alexandria said, to "the great number of illnesses" we have, which we believed were innocuous tastes and habits: "the love of meat on the table, of wine, of women, the libertine lifestyle and every kind of pleasure-seeking: and above all reigns concupiscence. Alongside these things multiply, like sisters, numerous passions which, altogether, make up a libertine lifestyle".[2] It is a lifestyle in

1. Basil, *De ieiunio sermo I*, VII.
2. Clement of Alexandria, *Paedagogus*, II, 93, 2-3.

which human freedom is reduced to a minimum: everything that the subject does is dictated, not by him or herself, but by ingrained habits, by eating fads, by lust, greed, fear and attachment.

Once we have become aware of our lack of freedom, of our non-freedom, we then have to undertake a spiritual process to reacquire our freedom. This process is generally known as ascetic discipline (from the Greek *askesis,* training), in which fasting plays an important role. This process consists largely in practising the renunciation of pleasures, so that we learn to be able to manage without them. We do this, and this is an important point, not because these things are in themselves bad, but simply because too often we are dependent on them, conditioned by them, subjugated by them. Thus it is important to train ourselves to do without them, so that we become masters and no longer slaves, of pleasures, sensations and emotions. This is why we should not just abstain from meat on fast days, but also from all rich foods and delicacies (cf Daniel 10: 3).[3] Above all, we "should avoid those foods which, by seducing the appetite, cause us to

3. Cf Jerome, Epistolae, CVIII, 17.

eat even when we are not hungry",[4] as often happens. On fast days, but not only on fast days, we should be content with any "food that we have to hand"; "Lenten observance" and every fast should in fact be "a brake on our old desires" and not, by seeking out special foods, "the chance [to try out] for new pleasures".[5]

The Fathers also suggest practising asceticism with regard to drinking, including restraining a little our desire to drink water,[6] and not to eat until we are completely satisfied, but to stop beforehand. Above all they suggest giving up the bad habit of always having something in our mouths, or of drinking and eating, every time we feel the urge to, biscuits, sweets, crisps, and the like. Not only is this unhealthy, but it is also a sign of a complete lack of self-discipline and self-mastery. And all this should be done, as we have already noted, "not for the superstition of observing a law," Origen reminds us, "but for the virtue of self-control".[7] If we want to be someone who remains faithful to his or her spouse and able

4. *Clement of Alexandria, Paedagogus, II, 15, 1.*
5. *Augustine, Sermones, CCVII, 2.*
6. *Cf Talassius Libicus, Centuriae, IV, 33.*
7. Origen, *In Leviticum homiliae*, X, 2.

to resist the attraction of a face, a body or a voice, we will first have to learn how to resist the smell of roast beef. In this sense, "fasting is a school of self-control", says Ambrose.[8]

It is clear, therefore, that self-control, in this sense, is a fundamental virtue, and that fasting is just one of the ways of achieving it. St Ephraem, one of the great Fathers of the Church, explains this very well: "There is self-control of the tongue: not speaking useless or superfluous words, not speaking ill of others, not cursing, not using vulgar expressions, not sowing discord, accusing one's neighbour, not divulging secrets or being curious about our neighbour's business. There is self-control of the hearing: not listening to useless things. There is self-control of the eyes: being master of what one chooses to look at, not seeking out or dwelling on sensuous or indecent things. There is self-control of the temper: to master one's anger, so as not to explode in an instant [...]. There is self-control regarding food: not overeating or not eating delicacies, not eating between meals, not letting oneself be the victim of greed or be drawn by the pleasure of looking

8. Ambrose, De Elia et ieiunio, VIII (22).

at beautiful dishes, or continually desire different foods. There is self-control with regard to drinking: keep a check on one's consumption of wine, do not be drawn by the desire to taste vintage wines or to drink too much wine, do not be looking continually for different drinks or the attraction of artificial drinks..."[9]

And in the same vein, fast days are also, for married people, days on which to abstain from conjugal relationships,[10] something which is recommended for the same reasons as abstaining from food. The expression "fast day" means the period "between one evening and the following evening" (Leviticus 23: 32), starting and ending with "the setting of the sun" (cf 2 Samuel 3: 35), in compliance with Biblical and Early Christian tradition. In the modern Church, the period of fasting is regarded as being from the beginning of the day until midnight.

But let us return to the subject of the usefulness of the discipline of fasting. We have seen how advantageous it is for the human person to impose limits on him or herself and to practice renunciation. It is also very helpful

9. Ephraem, *Sermo XXII de continentia* (in the Greek version).
10. Cf *Augustine, Sermones*, CCV, 2; CCIX, 3.

to follow the formal "rules" laid down by the Church. St Basil says: "Is it good to decide to abstain from certain foods and drinks for a period of time? [...] No, because any decision taken according to one's own will is dangerous";[11] "in fact, temperance does not consist in abstaining from material foods [...] but in a complete abstention from one's own will".[12] Thus it is very helpful if we simply follow the rules of the Christian tradition so that we minimise the creativity and the exuberance of our own will, as it is this that we are really trying to dominate and discipline.

So, we can see that the most serious thing with regard to fasting is not so much "to take food, as to break the rule",[13] because the aim is not to lose weight or damage oneself, but to master one's own will and to be able to respect a discipline, when the passions, that is the desires of the will, the habits and impulses of the body, are urging us to do otherwise.

This is one of the reasons why the Church establishes precise days in which it is obligatory to fast, and lays down precise rules which we

11. Basil, *Regulae brevius tractatae,* CXXXVII.
12. Ibid., *CXXVIII.*
13. John Cassian, *Collationes,* XXI, 14.

are obliged to obey. If fasting was left to each one's personal decision, greed, hunger, laziness and other passions would lead us easily to do fasts which are more convenient for us, making them innocuous and, in the end, useless.

The aim of Christian asceticism is to weaken the power the passions have over us, in the first place desire, greed and attachment to oneself. Each of us, in fact, is under the influence of a continual "desiring which, when we give in to it, in order to satisfy it, is revived and becomes even stronger".[14] What happens, as Lucretius explains, "from the very heart of the pleasures arises a strange bitterness which, in the midst of the fruits of the crime, creates anxiety".[15] In other words, the mind is constantly building up cravings: "The appetite of the lazy craves, and gets nothing" (Proverbs 13: 4). When we obtain something, we become attached to it and start to resist everything which threatens our possession of it. Continuously tossed around by irrational passions, we are in a state of constantly wanting what we do not have. But "every time man desires something inordinately, he

14. Clement of Alexandria, Stromata, III, 41, 6.
15. Lucretius, De rerum natura, IV, 1133-1134.

immediately feels a lack of inner peace [...] and if someone opposes him, he becomes upset for nothing [...]. Thus it is only by resisting the passions that we find true peace, not by supporting them".[16] This is why "fasting is better than prayer",[17] because it "kills concupiscence and, together with prayer, purifies the mind".[18]

At this point, however, we must make a distinction: when fasting is practised as total abstinence from food for many hours, or for a whole day, or for several days, it puts us in touch with a fundamental element in our life: suffering. Whoever has observed total prolonged fasts (for example for three days or a week) knows very well that after a certain length of time one has a feeling of general tiredness and also pain in the stomach. As time goes on, the tiredness increases; we get a headache and start to feel drowsy. Often this state of weakness makes us tense and prone to lose our temper. We feel especially that we don't have the strength to do our normal work and that we are "wasting time".

16. *De imitatione Christi*, I, 6.
17. *II Epistola Clementis*, XVI, 4.
18. Maximus the Confessor, *Capita de charitatae*, I, 79. Also Basil, *De ieiunio sermo I*, VI.

In the meantime, hunger pangs are affecting us. We start to go round in a bad mood, intolerant of others. We start to look for excuses to break our fast. "Perhaps I'm not strong enough," "maybe it's bad for my health," "why should I punish myself like this?" are all thoughts which come into our head. But we also realise that a new dimension is emerging from within us and that we are coming into a deeper contact with ourselves. It's like entering into an underground canal which takes us deeper and deeper down. We begin to understand what the Bible says: "He humbled you by letting you hunger, then by feeding you with manna [...] in order to make you understand that one does not live by bread alone, but by every word that comes from the mouth of the Lord." (Deuteronomy 8: 3, Matthew 4: 4). A prolonged fast takes us beyond our normal daily routine and into a different world. It is a mystical experience of leaving behind our normal selves to find a deeper, unfamiliar self.

Then the tiredness, the nausea and the exhaustion are so bad that we can neither pray nor do any other spiritual task. We find ourselves simply before our own suffering. But even then it is important not to break our fast, because these feelings pass and also because they have a great spiritual value, inasmuch as they help us experience the "dark night" and the "desert" of the heart. After all, observes Isaac of Nineveh, "it is better stopping spiritual practices because of fasting, rather than because of the heaviness we feel through overeating",[19] which is more often the case. Throughout our lives, says St Basil, we are very good at killing our bodies through eating too much, or eating unhealthy foods; so, it would do us good for our body to suffer a little through a healthy fast![20]

And while we are suffering stomach cramps, a new feeling of closeness to Christ in his sorrowful passion arises within us. We start to understand what suffering is and what Jesus' suffering on Calvary meant for us. Every pang of hunger reminds us of Christ and of that God for whom we are fasting. Also, the hunger and the exhaustion break our attachment to the passions which have such a strong hold over us on this earth. Now, suddenly, we start to feel indifference towards and annoyance with those pleasures that, normally, govern the whole of our existence. We raise our eyes heavenwards and start to long for a new Earth and a new homeland. We see death

19. Isaac of Nineveh, *De perfectione religiosa*, XXXV.
20. Basil, *De ieiunio sermo I*, IV.

too in a new light: it is the angel whom God will send to call us to leave this passing world, whose attractions are not as exciting or marvellous as we thought before our fast.

"Fasting is food for the mind."[21] In our day-to-day lives in fact, while we are continuously concerned with eating, eating well and eating plenty, "your mind and your soul," says St Basil, "are made hungry through lack of spiritual food".[22] After one or two days of fasting we are different to what we usually are: although we are suffering, we find a new peace. In fact, the pain of fasting, because it is so insistent, cannot be endured if we do not keep our minds continuously aware of our body and its discomfort. In this way, says St Nilus of Ancyra, fasting also becomes "fasting from thoughts".[23] St John Chrysostom says that "thanks to our continuous reminding of God, we are able to control our wandering thoughts which are always in action."[24] St Ambrose notes that "fasting loves stillness", whereas normal daily lives are hectic

21. Ambrose, *De Elia et ieiunio,* III (4).
22. Basil, *De ieiunio sermo I,* IX.
23. Nilus of Ancyra, *Epistolae,* IV, 3.
24. John Chrysostom, Homilia V de ieiunio et in Joniam prophetam, IV. Cf also Isaac of Nineveh, Sermones ascetici, LXXXV (Greek version).
25. John Cassian, *De coenobiorum institutes,* V, 10.

and frenetic.[25] Normally, after a day or two, the stomach cramps cease, as does the feeling of hunger, as does the initial discomfort and you begin to get a "taste" for this new "spiritual food".

The "struggle" of the fast, as it is often described by Christian tradition, is nevertheless tiring and difficult: every hour that passes without eating is an interior battle: it is a little taste of the battle Jesus faced during his forty days in the desert: "for forty days he was tempted by the devil. He ate nothing at all during those days" (Luke 4: 2). Isaac of Nineveh says that "the work of fasting precedes any struggle against sin and its desires... it is the start of the way of Christianity".[26] Jesus himself said that certain demons "can only be cast out with prayer and with fasting" (Matthew: 17: 20, Vulgate).

Only by trying it out for yourself can you experience the extreme fatigue and the inexpressible beauty of fasting.

26. Isaac of Nineveh, *De perfectione religiosa*, XXXV.

Chapter 4

Fasting as Purification

Summing up what has been said in the preceding chapters, we can say that there are three aspects of Christian fasting: fasting is a sign of mourning and penance, or at least of respect, in front of God; it is a form of solidarity and sharing with the poor, and expresses the Christian option of poverty; it is a discipline which consists in practising renunciation to free oneself from the slavery of passions and desires. A fourth basic aspect can be added to these three: fasting is a way of purifying our psycho-physical organism.

Although today this latter aspect is virtually ignored by the Catholic Church, the Tradition of the Church, right from the earliest times, adopted the Greco-Roman concept of dieting and fasting as instruments for ensuring bodily health. Fasting is *"alimentum salutis"*;[1] fasting

1. *Ambrose, De Elia et ieiunio, VIII (22).*

"is good for health".[2] But why should religion be interested in this idea? The answer is that bodily health is not far removed from religion, for the following two reasons: because, as St Basil says, to apply God's commandments to one's life and to everything expected of a good Christian, good health is necessary;[3] and because bodily health is inextricably linked to the health, the clarity, and the peace of the mind, and therefore to the whole interior life. A person who suffers from nervous tension, digestive problems, migraine, hormonal imbalance etc., will find it difficult to reflect, to meditate, to pray.

The physiological and therapeutic character of fasting is constantly emphasised by the Fathers of the Church, and especially by the Greek Fathers. St Basil says that fasting improves digestion and contributes in many ways to one's health. "Human bodies," he says, "weighed down by continuous overeating, easily fall prey to illness".[4] St John Chrysostom too uses medical terminology: "Fasting is a medicine. But medicine, even though it is useful for one's health, can become useless

2. Basil, *Regulae fusius tractatae,* XVIII.
3. Ibid. XIX, 2; John Cassian, *De coenoborium institutes,* V, 8.
4. Basil, *De ieiunio sermo I,* IV; cf Also ibid., IX.

because of the inexperience of the person using it. We have to know for how long we should take it, as well as the quantity required, the constitution of the body taking it, the nature of the place, the season of the year, the correct regime of the diet and many other factors. If we overlook one of these, all our preparations will be ruined".[5] Still today in the Greek Orthodox Church this aspect of fasting is very much present in its teaching. "Fasting," writes a contemporary Greek bishop, is "an ideal method of detoxicating the human organism and of preventing various illnesses," it contributes to "the lowering of cholesterol, the prevention of heart attacks and of certain types of tumour".[6]

All of this does not just apply to fasting itself, but to all dietary regimes. One of the Fathers particularly interested in this subject is St Clement of Alexandria (second century), whose observations merit being quoted in this book.

"Food should be simple and unsophisticated [...]; the food which is best for one's health and strength is certainly that which can

5. *John Chrysostom, Homilia III in descessum Flaviani episcopi.*
6. *Symeon Koutsa, I nistia tis Ekklesias, Athens, 2003, pp. 43-44.*

be obtained easily, is easy to digest and is light"; he issues a warning about "fried foods, desserts made with honey, and cakes". He continues: "The body, by nature, gains no advantage from overeating; in fact, the opposite is true, those who eat very frugally are stronger, healthier and more beautiful [...]. And they are not only physically more vigorous, but they are also mentally more lucid [...]: in fact their intellect is not clouded by food or blinded by the pleasures of the senses [...]. So, let our meal be frugal and light, in order that we can stay awake, let it also not be complicated by too many courses [...]. A diet that goes beyond what is necessary is not good for us, clouds the mind and makes the body weak and susceptible to illnesses". Further on, Clement, having said that it is good "to vary our foods" – "as long as we don't exhaust ourselves doing it", continues saying: "A lot of food generates sickness in the soul and a loss of memory and intelligence; also, the bodies of growing children develop best if their eating is contained". And finally he says: "The belching of someone who has filled himself with wine, the snoring of someone who has stuffed himself with food and is lying between the covers, the rumbling of overworked stomachs – all this ruins the calm clarity of the eye of the soul, and the mind is packed with thousands of images and fantasies".[7]

In many societies the use of food and fasting has also been associated with "magic" and ecstatic phenomena. Tertullian, for example, noted that fasting caused dreams.[8] In fact, it is known that prolonged fasting or the eating of certain foods, such as some mushrooms, can induce "visions" and paranormal states. We must emphasise here that in Christian Tradition it has never been the aim to induce such phenomena. On the contrary, the Christian Tradition on fasting aims at "freeing [the mind] from dreamlike images", from strange thoughts, emotions and fantasies, and making it more clear and self-aware. Fasting, says St John Climacus, is "a medicine which purifies us from passions"[9]. St Augustine says that our heart can turn to God in prayer only if it is not "impeded by cloudy fantasies caused by carnal desires".[10] And the New Testament always links sobriety with mental vigilance and awareness (cf 1 Thessalonians 5: 6; 1 Peter 1: 13; 5: 8).

7. Clement of Alexandria, *Paedagogus,* II, 2, 1; II, 4, 1; II, 5, 2; II, 7, 3; II, 10, 2; II, 17, 3; II, 81 1-2.
8. Tertullian, *De anima,* XXXVIII.
9. John Climacus, *Scala paradisi,* XIV and XXVI, 20.
10. Augustine, *Sermones,* CCVII, 3.

The diet we are describing here and the practice of fasting help us live chastity. "The satisfaction of the stomach stimulates the libido".[11] Both experience and science show, in fact, that overeating (especially of meat and similar foods) increases the production of sperm in men, which in turn increases libido. In this way sexuality becomes difficult to control: "So, let us keep a check on our stomach, in order to keep a check on that which is below the stomach," says St Cyril of Jerusalem.[12]

It is important to let the stomach rest and not to eat continuously, that is, in between meals. On fast days this means waiting until 15.00 or until evening time before eating,[13] avoiding all food until that time. According to ancient tradition, even drinking water is not permitted,[14] which is what Muslims still do during Ramadan. On non-fast days we should not eat more than two or three meals, without taking tea breaks, snacks and the like.[15] To control our eating in this way, by observing "a

11. Anthony the Great, *Epistolae,* I, 4.
12. Cyril of Jerusalem, *Homilia in paralyticum,* XVIII; also Nilus of Ancira, *Liber de monastica.*
13. Cf Benedict of Nursia, *Regula,* XLI; Basil, *De ieiunio sermo I,* IX; John Cassian, *De coenoborium institutes,* V, 5, 2.
14. *Apophthegmata patrum* (alphabetical series), Silvanus, I.
15. Cf John Cassian, *De coenoborium institutes,* V, 20.

measured fast every day", was judged by the Fathers to be more advantageous and better for our purification than long, drawn-out fasts of three or fours days, or a week.[16] These latter fasts are in fact much more difficult and painful and run the risk of creating tensions and being counter-productive.

Let us move on now to consider those foods which Christian tradition considers prohibited on fast days. First of all there is meat. In the early centuries of Christianity various philosophical and religious currents, especially Neo-Platonism and Pythagoreanism, forbade, as do various religions and sects today, the eating of meat. The Church was opposed to this rigorous vegetarian ideal, proclaiming officially that eating meat is not sinful and is permissible.[17] Nevertheless, very early on, the Christian ideal soon developed a vegetarian tendency: "We should not eat a lot of meat, because man is not a meat-eater, but a bread-eater".[18] Also St Paul says: "it is good not to eat meat or drink wine" (Romans 14: 21), and the Fathers reiterate unanimously that the heavy effect of meat

16. Idem. *Ad Castorem pontificem de octo pricipalibus vitiis*, I.
17. See for example Porphyrius, *De abstinentia ab esu cranium.*
18. Clement of Alexandria, *Paedagogus*, II, 55, 3; cf Ambrose, *De virginibus*, III, 8 (2); Isidore of Seville, *De ecclesiasticis officiis*, XLV, 1.

"obscures the soul".[19] Thus reducing the consumption of meat was always on the agenda; for monks it was totally prohibited for the whole of their lives,[20] and for lay people it was strictly prohibited on fast days. Making connections with the Greek vegetarian traditions already mentioned and also with Plato, the Fathers began to define the doctrine of the Church ever more precisely[21] At the beginning of creation, say the Fathers, God gave only vegetables to man and woman (Genesis 1: 29) and we should abide by this rule. Meat expresses killing, blood, cruelty and an act of violence against nature, says St Basil.[22] It is not good for our health, makes the body heavy and clouds the mind, and the protein it contains can be found in other foods (especially vegetables).

It is important to remember that, as in many of the ancient civilisations, also in the Bible and in the Greco-Roman world, meat had sacred and sacrificial connotations. Above all, it was the priests who ate meat after sacrificing the victims on the altar. The act of killing a living being and eating its flesh is something that puts one very

19. Clement of Alexandria, *Paedagogus*, II, 11, 1.
20. Cf Benedict of Nursia, *Regula*, XXXIX.
21. Cf Plato, *Timaeus*, XXXIII, 80e; cf Also Seneca, *Epistolae morales*, CVIII.
22. Cf Basil, *De ieiunio sermo I*, Vii.

much in contact with the mystery of life and of death and was therefore always seen as something sacred and religious. Still today in Islam, in Ethiopian Christianity and in other traditions, the slaughter of animals is subject to a precise religious ritual.

This form of meat eating with its priestly and sacrificial character meant that meat was considered to be a very prestigious food, in the first place by the warrior and aristocratic classes, then later by all. If we reflect on the fact that eating meat is a rite of contact with death, we will come to realise why in the early Christian tradition it was not considered to be a dish like any other, but was eaten solely at Easter and on other sacred days, as a sacred and symbolic act linked to the sacrifice of the body of Christ and to his death and resurrection.

Another food forbidden on fast days was fish, as it too is the flesh of living beings. However, because it is not as difficult to digest or as damaging to the organism, eating it was always considered a less serious "offence". Around the seventh century, the Latin Church removed it from the list of foods prohibited on fast days,[23] and the Orthodox Church, while

23. Cf Rabanus Maurus, *De institutione clericorum,* II, 27; Thomas Aquinas, *Summa theologica,* II-II, 147, 8.

still maintaining the ban on fish, allows seafood such as squid and other "fish without blood" to be eaten.

Like all other foods created by God, wine too is allowed for the Christian. Even the most austere of the Fathers of the Church consider wine to be not only permissible, but actually good for health if taken in small doses and duly watered down.[24] St Benedict even allowed his monks to drink wine.[25] Nevertheless, they were also well aware of the dangers of drinking too much wine. It comes as no surprise therefore to discover that wine, and other alcoholic drinks, were forbidden on fast days.[26] It was not until about the X century that the Latin Church started to allow it.[27]

Eggs and dairy products were also prohibited on fast days. This is due to their animal derivations and the Church forbade them for the same reasons as for meat. In the seventh century the Council in Trullo reconfirmed the ban on eggs and dairy products for the whole of Lent,[28] as did Thomas Aquinas several centuries

24. Cf Clement of Alexandria, *Paedagogus,* II, 23; cf 1 Tm 5, 23.
25. Benedict of Nursia, *Regula,* XL.
26. Cf Basil, *De ieiunio sermo I,* VII and IX; Maximus of Turin, *Sermones,* XVIII; cf Dan 10: 3.
27. *Cf Thomas Aquinas, Summa theologica,* II-II, 147, 8.
28. Council in Trullo, can. LVI.

later.[29] This ruling is still in force in the Eastern Churches, and not just during Lent, but on all fast days, therefore every Wednesday and Friday. In fact, the practice was only officially abolished by the Catholic Church in the twentieth century.

Fasting, at least during Lent, also excluded oil, especially olive oil. This tradition, mentioned by St Jerome in the fourth century and by St Isidore[30] in the sixth, was abandoned quite early on by the Catholic Church but is still kept in the Orthodox Church. Why a ban on oil? There are two basic reasons: the purification of the body, which is one of the purposes of fasting, requires the elimination of anything fatty or fried; olive oil also has symbolic connotations. Olive oil and wine are symbols of joy and celebration (cf Psalm 104: 15) which have been made in sacred symbols by the Church through their use in the sacraments. Thus oil and wine were reserved for feast days and are forbidden on fast days.

Another example of symbolism with regard to food is honey. This should be avoided

29. Cf Thomas Aquinas, *Summa theologica*, II-II, 147, 8.
30. Cf Jerome, *Epistolae*, CVIII, 17; Isidore of Seville, *Regula monachorum*, XII.

on fast days[31] both because of its animal origins and because it represents the joy of reaching the Promised Land of heaven which is "flowing with milk and honey" (Exodus 3: 8).

As well as the foods we have already spoken about, the Church also considers sophisticated dishes and delicacies, including vegetarian ones, and going to the theatre, to be against the penitential and ascetical spirit of Lent and of fast days. Nowadays, such things as smoking, television, cinema and excessive work activity, are also considered to be things to avoid on fast days.

All the dietary laws which have been explained in this chapter make up the so-called *xerophagia* regime. Xerophagia is a Greek word which means "dry eating" and implies total abstinence from the six forbidden foods (meat, fish, dairy products, eggs, wine and oil), as well as eating just one meal of uncooked food, and that after 15.00 hours. *Xerophagia* is still today observed on all 200 or so fast days in the Orthodox Church. Like modern-day vegans, the Fathers of the Church recommend applying *xerophagia* every day of our lives[32] (anyone

31. Cf Jerome, *Epistolae*, CVIII, 17.
32. Cf ibid.

intending to do this must make sure that they have a sufficient intake of proteins, minerals and vitamins). Nevertheless, all Christians were obliged to observe *xerophagia* for the whole of Lent from the Council of Laodicea in the fourth century.[33]

It is interesting to note that the distinction between foods that are compatible with xerophagia and those that are not can be found in many other religious traditions, as well as in modern dietary science. In India, for example, they talk about *sattvic* foods, those which are light, vegetarian, pure and conducive to contemplating the truth (*sattva*). In contrast, *rajasic* foods are heavy, greasy, fleshy and associated with irrational passions (*rajas*). In the Taoist tradition abstinence from "forbidden foods" was observed in order to purify the mind and achieve lucidity and concentration.

One final aspect, regarding fasting as detoxification and purification, has to do with the duration. It is obvious that if one practises xerophagia or a total fast for one day, and then the next one goes back to eating meat, eggs, wine etc., the benefits are extremely limited. This is why the Church, right from the earliest times, established, as well as individual fast

33. Council of Laodicea, can. L.

days, longer periods of rigorous fasting. The practice of the three-day, *triduum* fast, when absolutely nothing is eaten, was frequent and still exists in the Orthodox Church, although now only for monks. This total abstinence from food, which sometimes lasted five days or more, is undoubtedly an excellent method of detoxification. In fact, this was the fast that Moses, Elijah and Jesus himself did. "Moses was there with the Lord for forty days and forty nights; he neither ate bread nor drank water" (Exodus 34: 28; cf Deuteronomy 9: 9). St Basil says that "Fasting brought Elijah to be a spectator of the great Vision; in fact, having for forty days made his soul pure and chaste through fasting, he was consequently made worthy to accede to the grotto of Mount Horeb to see the Lord".[34]

In place of this total fast for forty days (biologically not impossible for a human being, but in reality only manageable by a few ascetics), the Church instituted the mitigated Lenten fast (i.e., *xerophagia*). The purifying and detoxifying nature of this fast (and other long fasts) was such that, although Saturdays and Sundays (or just Sundays) were considered

34. Basil, *De ieiunio sermo I*, VI.

feast days, the Church ruled that none of the prohibited foods should be eaten for the whole of Lent, except for a glass of wine and a drop of oil on Sundays (or also Saturdays) in order to recognise the festive character of that day. This ruling also meant that the penitential aspect of the fast was also maintained throughout the whole of Lent.

Chapter 5

Fasting in the Church's Teaching

In the preceding chapters we have illustrated and described traditional Christian teaching on the meaning and practice of fasting as it was intended and lived by the first and principal teachers of the Christian faith: the Apostles and the Fathers of the Church. It is clear, however, at least from the point of view of the Roman Catholic Church, that fasting nowadays is very different from that of the early Church, both in its methods and in its spirit. We may well ask ourselves: Why have all these rules about not eating eggs or milk, for example, or fasting on Wednesdays, been dropped? When did the change take place? Is it that the Church changed the rules, or that the people started to break them? Thus it will be necessary to dedicate a page or two to explaining the evolution of the practice of fasting down the centuries.

For the very first generations of Christians, as we have shown earlier in this book, there were three basic points regarding fasting: it was considered to be a very important element of the Christian faith; it was practised in a very austere way; it was not, initially, governed by precise and binding rules ("Priests fast when they so wish, as do the laity", wrote St Hippolytus at the start of the third century).[1]

However, very soon, the customs of the Apostolic era were transformed into fixed and binding rules regarding which days to fast, which foods were prohibited, and so on. At the same time, however, the Fathers, faced with a Christianity which often tended towards fanaticism and excesses with regard to fasting, continued to emphasise the fact that fasting is not an end in itself, but is a psychophysical good for the human person. Thus fasting was never to be regarded as absolute and should never endanger spiritual or physical health. Many people at that time observed such rigorous fasts that they often ruined their health, which consequently meant that in their spiritual lives they became sad and depressed. Therefore the Fathers were constantly reminding people to exercise wise discretion: "Fasts," says St Jerome, "should be moderate; if they are excessive, they ruin the stomach",[2] "prolonged abstinence from food saps the body's

1. Hippolytus, *Traditio apostolica,* XXIII.
2. Jerome, *Epistolae,* CXXV, 7.

vigour, weakening it in its spiritual work"[3] and makes the soul "sad and indifferent when speaking [about God]".[4] St Basil says: "People's needs differ according to their age, the work they do and their physical constitution", so eating should be "adapted to meet the needs of each person".[5] The sick and the infirm are exempt from fasting[6] and each one should fast "according to their ability to sustain it".[7] The pilgrim Egeria, visiting the Church in Palestine in the fourth century, writes: "No one must impose what should be done, but each one should do what they can. You should neither praise those who do more, nor blame those who do less".[8]

This spirit of toleration, albeit within the context of the seriousness and rigour with which fasting was practised, can be found in the attitude of the Fathers towards the different traditions of the various Churches. For example, already in the second century, in answer to Pope Victor who had excommunicated the Eastern Churches because they observed Lent

3. John Cassian, *Ad Castorem pontificem de octo principalibus vitiis,* I.
4. Diadocus of Foticea, *Capita centum de perfectione spirituali,* XLV.
5. Basil, *Regulae fusius tractatae,* XIX, 1.
6. Cf *Canones apostolorum,* LXIX.
7. Jerome, *Epistolae,* LII, 12.
8. Egeria, *Itinerarium,* XXVIII, 4.

differently from the Church of Rome, St Irenaeus wrote: "The criticism regarded not only the day, but the actual form of the fast. Some in fact believed that they had to fast for only one day, others for two, others even more [...]. And a similar difference of observance of fasting started, not in our time, but long ago, in the time of our predecessors who, it seems, without being over precise, confirmed this tradition in its simplicity and in its special character, and they laid it down for the future. None of them lived any less in peace, and we too live in peace with one another, and the difference in fasting confirms the consent of faith".[9]

St Augustine explains that, in the New Testament "we do not find it [...] explicitly commanded to observe fasts on certain precise days"; however, he says that in the Church "there is room for variety"; he goes on to tell how one day he asked his bishop, Ambrose of Milan, if it was right to observe the Saturday fast, like they did in Rome, or not, as was the custom in Milan and in the East. The bishop replied: "When I am here [in Milan], I do not fast on Saturday; when I am in Rome, I fast on Saturday; to whichever Church you go, observe their custom".[10] St Leo says: "we

9. Irenaeus of Lyons, in Eusebius of Caesaria, *Historia ecclesiastica*, V, 24, 12-13.
10. Augustine, *Epistolae*, XXXVI, 14 (32).

should not doubt that every Christian observance is taught by God, and everything the Church has adopted as a devout practice comes from the tradition of the Apostles and from the teaching of the Holy Spirit".[11] So, the key thing is not whether we should fast on Saturday or not, but that we respect the different practices of the Churches, as long as they are not "against the faith and good customs... and that the differences in observance are not the cause of schism".[12] St Augustine says that to condemn Eastern or Western-Roman practices would be both mistaken and presumptuous, also because Christ did not lay down any rules on this subject.[13] "Each province knows very well what to do, and therefore maintains its traditional rules as it does the apostolic laws", and "the custom of one Church is not affected by that observed by another".[14]

Given all of this, let us now have a brief look at how the practice of fasting has been modified in the Church, from the beginnings to the present day. We have seen what the

11. Leo I, *Sermones*, LXXIX (at LXXVII), 1.
12.Isidore of Seville, *De ecclesiasticis officiis*, II, 44.
13. Augustine, *Epistolae*, LXXXII, 2 (14).
14. Jerome, *Epistolae*, LXXI, 6.

rules for fasting were during the Patristic era (they were virtually identical in both East and West). These rules remain substantially the same in the Eastern Churches today, but in the Western Church there have been many significant changes.

An anonymous homily of the eighth century lists the various fast days and periods and reminds the congregation that fasting means, "abstaining from eating meat".[15] In fact, in the Latin world, fasting was soon reduced to abstaining from meat and from wine. Around about the seventh century, prohibitions on fish, oil,[16] eggs and dairy products (which remained forbidden during Lent) and, before the tenth century, also wine,[17] were progressively removed from customs and from ecclesiastical laws. In the meantime, while the Friday fast remained and the Saturday one was confirmed, the Wednesday fast became increasingly ignored, until it finally disappeared around

15. Homilia de decimus et de ieiunio (PL 129, 1261).

16. In 1351, Pope Clement VI decreed that fish and oil were allowed on fast days (Epistola Super quibusdam ad Consolatorem, Catholicon Armeniorum, n. XXXII.

17. Cf Rabanus Maurus (VIII-IX century), De institutione clericorum, II, 27: fasting, he says, is abstaining from meat and wine, but fish and game are permitted.

the eleventh century.[18] In the thirteenth century Thomas Aquinas, interpreting the Latin custom, which had already been consolidated and was to remain an authoritative reference point for many centuries to come, affirms that fasting consists solely of abstaining from meat (except in Lent when eggs and dairy products are also forbidden).[19] He also establishes the age of 21 years from which the faithful are obliged to fast, an age which was later included in Canon Law. In the early Church there was no age limit, and even children fasted as much as they were able. During the same period [thirteenth century] the custom developed of eating more than one meal a day on fast days, and also of eating *granite*[20] and other similar foods during the day.

From 1500 onwards popes started to issue Bulls which, as a reward for good service, granted "dispensations" to cities and whole

18. Cf Rabanus Maurus (VIII-IX century), *De institutione clericorum*, II, 23: he mentions Friday and Saturday as fast days. In the IX century, Pope Leo IV reminds the faithful that Wednesday is also a fast day (in: Corpus iuris canonici, *Decetum Gratiani*, III, 4, 11). We see in the Rule of St Francis, for example, that Wednesday and not Friday, is mentioned (*I Regula* III, 15-16).
19. Thomas Aquinas, *Summa theologica*, II-II, 147, 8.
20. A grainy-textured, flavoured water ice.

regions allowing them for example to eat eggs and milk during Lent, or lard, or even meat. This relaxation of the rules on fasting reached the point where the popes themselves started to be alarmed. In 1741, Benedict XIV wrote: "We cannot fail to regret that the most sacred observance of the Lenten fast, through the excessive and indiscriminate granting of dispensations everywhere, for futile and not urgent reasons, has been almost entirely eliminated".[21] A few years later, in an Encyclical specially dedicated to the subject of fasting, Pope Benedict bemoans the situation once again: "It has happened that in some cities and dioceses all the faithful, already for many years and without any distinction, eat meat during Lent!"[22]

The Church tried to stem the tide, but without success. Catholics no longer understood the meaning of fasting as intended by the early Fathers. Great Doctors of the Church like Francis de Sales and Alphonsus Liguori did not recognise the importance attributed to fasting in the past. The emphasis was now on other values: obedience to superiors, humility

21. Benedict XIV, *Brief Non ambigimus* (1741), n. 1.
22. Idem. *Encyclical Libentissime* (1745), n. 10.

towards the hierarchical Church, works of charity, Eucharistic and Marian devotion. In 1874 the great moral theologian Peter Scavini reiterated the obligation of fasting according to traditional doctrine, more or less following the line of Thomas Aquinas's teaching. He noted (and approved of) however, the numerous dispensations and exceptions. Based on pontifical and Vatican decrees or authoritative theologians like St Alphonsus, Scavini explains, for example, that on fast days, not only are tea, coffee, sorbets, wine and cocoa permitted, but also breakfast with bread and hot chocolate. He also conceded that the line to follow was that of local tradition and the dispensations granted by the local bishop, even when this meant being allowed to eat meat during Lent or not to fast at all. Also, referring to authoritative documents he reminded the faithful that many categories of people were exempt from fasting: manual workers, doctors, lawyers, singers, writers, as well as men over sixty and women over fifty years of age.

At the dawn of the twentieth century, Pope Pius X promulgated new norms for the Church[23] which, theoretically, remained in

23. Cf Major Catechism, n. 483-493, and Code of Canon Law (of Pius X), can. 1250-1254.

force until the Second Vatican Council. Every Friday and Saturday (except with dispensation) the eating of meat was forbidden ("except in case of necessity"); on fast days, as well as lunch, breakfast and supper were allowed, "according to the approved custom of the place." Meat was forbidden, "but not eggs, dairy products and any type of condiment, even if made with animal fat"; fast days were, Ash Wednesday, Fridays and Saturdays in Lent (on other days in Lent meat eating was allowed), the Ember Days, the Eves of Pentecost, All Saints, the Assumption and Christmas; however, many exceptions and dispensations mitigated these rules to a considerable extent.

Now let us look at what the Roman Catholic Church says today about fasting. The Second Vatican Council does not have much to say about fasting apart from a brief reference to Good Friday, whose fast "must be kept sacred" and "should be celebrated everywhere".[24] Nor does the Catechism of the Catholic Church give any further indications about fasting.[25] There is an important

24. Second Vatican Council, Sacrosanctum Concilium, n. 110.
25. Cf *Catechism of the Catholic Church,* n. 1438.

Episcopal Note of 1994 directed to the Italian Church: *The Christian meaning of fasting and abstinence*. With reference to Pope Paul VI's Apostolic Constitution *Paenitemini* (1966) and Canons 1250-1253 of the new Code of Canon Law, this document sets out clearly the current rules on fasting.

1. The law on fasting stipulates "that only one meal should be eaten during the day, but does not prohibit a small amount of food being eaten in the morning and in the evening, taking into consideration the approved local custom regarding the quantity and quality".

2. The law of abstinence prohibits meat, as well as food and drinks which, having made a prudent judgement, are considered exotic and expensive.

3. Fasting and abstinence as explained above, must be observed on Ash Wednesday (or on the first Friday of Lent for the Ambrosian Rite), and on the Friday of the Passion and Death of Our Lord Jesus Christ; fasting and abstinence is also recommended on Holy Saturday, until the Easter Vigil.

4. Abstinence should be observed every Friday during Lent, unless it coincides with a Solemnity (like 19 and 25 March). On all the other Fridays of the year, unless a Solemnity, abstinence should be observed either as previously described, or by doing some other charitable work, by prayer or an act of charity.

5. All adults up to the beginning of their sixtieth year are obliged to follow these laws; the law of abstinence also applies to anyone who is fourteen years of age or above.

6. For a good reason, such as health for example, the obligations of fasting and abstinence may be waived. Also "the parish priest, for a good reason and in conformity with views of the diocesan bishop, may dispense with the obligation to observe the day (...) of penance, or he may commute it to other pious works" (n. 13).

As regards the Eucharistic fast, the current law is as follows: "Whoever is to receive the blessed Eucharist is to abstain for at least one hour before Holy Communion from all food and drink, with the sole exception of water and medicine".[26] The

26. Code of Canon Law (1983), can. 919.

time is reduced to a quarter of an hour for the sick, the elderly or those who care for them, or for their relatives, if they wish to receive the Eucharist with them and it would be inconvenient for them to observe an hour's fast.

As we can see, the Catholic Church's current rules on fasting are extremely bland and lacking in the ascetical rigour of the early Church. In fact, the Church has chosen to emphasise other forms of asceticism and "fasting" which it regards as much more important and more urgent. The Episcopal Note we have already quoted above lists the "foods" from which men and women today should abstain, at least during Lent:

> "eating foods with no restraint, sometimes accompanied by an intolerable waste of resources;
> the excessive consumption of alcoholic drinks and tobacco;
> the incessant search for superfluous things, accepting uncritically every fashion and every invitation to buy, made by commercial advertisers;
> often spending huge amounts of money on celebrations and even on religious functions;
> an unrestrained search for forms of entertainment which do not help us to rest either mentally or physically, but which are an

end in themselves and lead us to escape from reality and from our responsibilities; frenetic activity which leaves no space for silence, reflection and prayer; excessive use of television and other means of communication, which can make us dependent on them, can be an obstacle to personal reflection and impede dialogue within the family" (n. 11).

These words express concepts which are undoubtedly close to those of the early Fathers and are a sincere exhortation to live a more authentic form of Christianity, one which is more resistant to the seductions of the world and of secularisation, even though this "asceticism" is no longer concentrated on the traditional form of fasting.

It is important to note, at this point, that the Church has never forbidden the faithful to fast in the traditional way, and still today it can be both permitted and salutary, after consulting with one's spiritual director or bishop, to practise those more radical forms of fasting recommended by the Fathers of the Church and described in this book.

For the rest, as we have seen, still today, at the beginning of the third millennium, millions of faithful of the Eastern Churches fast with all the rigour of the early centuries of Christianity.

The Protestant Churches, which to begin with were very severe in the practice of fasting, today have virtually abandoned it, leaving it up to individual initiative. The Anglicans, and in part also the Armenian Church, have introduced changes in parallel with the Catholic Church. The Eastern Churches on the other hand (the Orthodox, the Copts of Egypt and Ethiopia, the Jacobites of Syria and the Nestorians) have maintained the ancient discipline, in the knowledge that they are united together in faithfulness to an age-old tradition, as the Coptic bishop Ibn al-Muqaffa' observed in the tenth century: "Our predecessors have passed these rules on to us, which they in their turn had received from their predecessors and so on, right back to the first [Christian] generation".[27]

It is interesting to see how in modern, secularised countries such as Greece, the discipline of fasting has remained virtually unchanged since the time of the Fathers of the Church, even though, obviously, only a small proportion of the faithful really adhere completely to those austere rules. It does not seem out of place, as we are speaking about

27. Severus Ibn al-Muqaffa', *Misbah al-Aql,* X.

the Orthodox Churches, to quote the words of the then Cardinal Joseph Ratzinger: "To fast means to accept an essential element of Christian life. We need to rediscover the corporeal aspect of faith: abstaining from food is one of these aspects [...], and for this we must look for an example to our brothers of the Eastern Orthodox Churches, great masters – still today – of authentic Christian asceticism".[28]

28. J. Ratzinger, *Rapporto sulla fede*, Ed. San Paolo, 1985 (1998), pp. 115-116.
(*The Ratzinger Report* - Ignatius Press, 1987)